AF506090

PICASSO | ENCOUNTERS

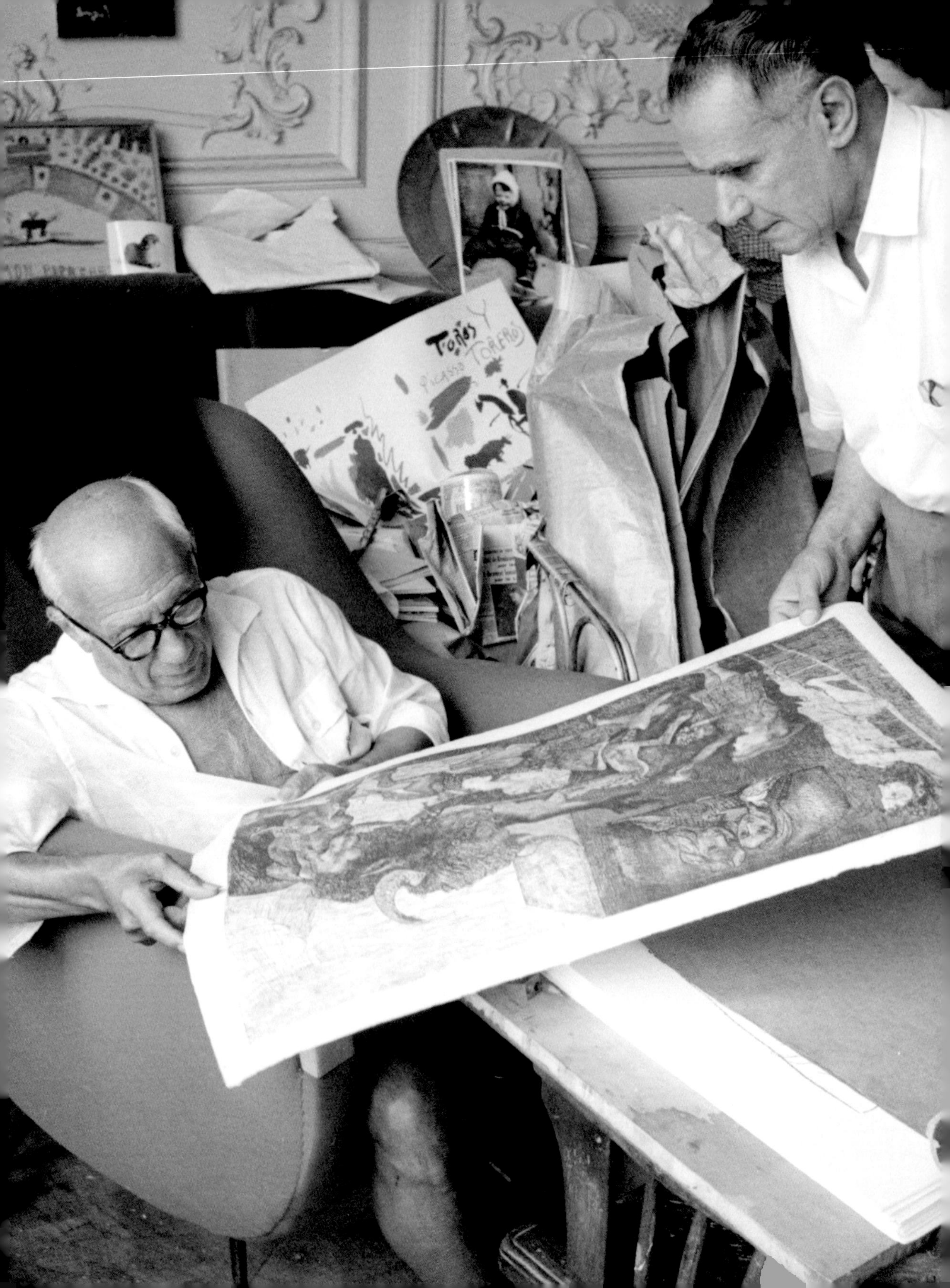

PICASSO | ENCOUNTERS

Jay A. Clarke and Marilyn McCully

Clark Art Institute
Williamstown, Massachusetts

Distributed by Yale University Press
New Haven and London

Published by the Clark Art Institute on the occasion of the exhibition *Picasso | Encounters*, Clark Art Institute, Williamstown, Massachusetts, June 4–August 27, 2017

Picasso | Encounters is organized by the Clark Art Institute, with the exceptional support of the Musée national Picasso-Paris. Additional support for the exhibition is provided by Margaret and Richard Kronenberg and Marilyn and Ron Walter.

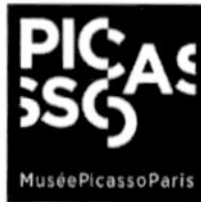

Produced by the Publications Department of the Clark Art Institute, 225 South Street, Williamstown, Massachusetts 01267
Anne Roecklein, Managing Editor
Kevin Bicknell, Assistant Editor and Rights Coordinator
Ashton Fancy, Publications Assistant
Jessica Rosenthal, Publications Intern

Copyedited by Sharon Herson
Designed by Roy Brooks, Fold Four, Inc., Milwaukee, Wisconsin
Proofread by Lucy Gardner Carson
Printed on McCoy Matte
Printed by Kirkwood Printing, Wilmington, Massachusetts

Cover: *The Weeping Woman, 1* (detail), 1937. Private collection

Details, photographs by Edward Quinn (Irish, 1920–1997):

p. 2: Picasso and Henri Matarasso, gallery owner and publisher, checking the etching *Minotauromachia*. La Californie, Cannes, 1961.

p. 12: Picasso and Françoise Gilot with sculpture *Head of Françoise*. Vallauris, 1953.

p. 34: Picasso, printer Jacques Frélaut, and painter Édouard Pignon. La Californie, Cannes, March 16, 1961.

pp. 54–55: Picasso with Hidalgo Arnéra and Piero Crommelynck. Notre-Dame-de-Vie, Mougins, 1964.

Distributed by Yale University Press, 302 Temple Street, P.O. Box 209040, New Haven, Connecticut 06520-9040
yalebooks.com/art

Printed and bound in the United States of America
10 9 8 7 6 5 4 3 2 1

Library of Congress Cataloging-in-Publication Data

Names: Clarke, Jay A. (Jay Anne). Picasso's creative collaborations. | McCully, Marilyn. Picasso and printmaking. | Picasso, Pablo, 1881–1973. Prints. Selections. | Sterling and Francine Clark Art Institute, organizer, host institution.
Title: Picasso | encounters / Jay A. Clarke and Marilyn McCully.
Description: Williamstown, Massachusetts : Clark Art Institute, 2017. | "Published by the Clark Art Institute on the occasion of the exhibition Picasso | Encounters, Clark Art Institute, Williamstown, Massachusetts, June 4–August 27, 2017." | Includes bibliographical references.
Identifiers: LCCN 2017014312 | ISBN 9781935998297 (clark art institute) | ISBN 9780300229271 (yale university press)
Subjects: LCSH: Picasso, Pablo, 1881–1973— Exhibitions.
Classification: LCC NE650.P62 A4 2017 | DDC 759.4— dc23 LC record available at https://lccn.loc.gov /2017014312

CONTENTS

FOREWORD

Chance encounters, lasting connections, transformative reunions: history is often read in regard to our relationships to others, both personal and professional. While popular mythology often idealizes artists who appear to create in solitude, with nothing but their own imaginations as inspiration, most are impacted by a host of companions in order to bring their work to life. *Picasso | Encounters* explores the relationships that famed Spanish artist Pablo Picasso formed during his life and how these connections shaped the course of his artistic career. Featuring thirty-eight of his most important prints and paintings, the exhibition focuses on major statements in Picasso's printmaking process.

The second exhibition to be held in the Michael Conforti Pavilion, *Picasso | Encounters* showcases the unique abilities of the space to adapt to various media. The exhibition also presents an opportunity to highlight aspects of the Clark's own exceptional collection of prints, many of which have been acquired through our encounters with collectors. Picasso's *The Frugal Repast* (1904), one of the artist's first attempts at printmaking, came to the Clark through the Herbert Leon Michel collection. Michel, a Chicago-based physician, amassed a great collection of late nineteenth-century French, Norwegian, Belgian, and Spanish prints after World War II, which he sold to the Clark in 1968 with the guidance of his dear friend and Art Institute of Chicago curator Harold Joachim, a close associate of the Clark's first director, Peter Guille—a series of serendipitous encounters that have inspired thousands more through the collection's use in exhibitions and scholarly study.

The Clark is fortunate to present this exhibition with the collaboration of the Musée national Picasso-Paris, which has lent two exceptional paintings: *Self Portrait* (late 1901) and *Portrait of Dora Maar* (1937). These works anchor the show's narratives within the greater biography of Picasso. In addition, we are grateful for the important works lent by the Metropolitan Museum of Art; the Museum of Modern Art; the Philadelphia Museum of Art; the Museum of Fine Arts, Boston; the John Szoke Gallery; Catherine Woodard and Nelson Blitz, Jr.; and those collectors who wish to remain anonymous.

I extend my thanks to Jay A. Clarke, Manton Curator of Prints, Drawings, and Photographs, for her curatorial vision. Her essay in this catalogue approaches Picasso's creative collaborations from a new and timely perspective, and her commitment to the project has created an exceptional display across the artist's career. Marilyn McCully's essay constitutes an important contribution to the history of Picasso's printers. Her attention to the exhibition's development and her support have strengthened the show's historical underpinnings. This exhibition would not be possible without the generous support of Margaret and Richard Kronenberg and Marilyn and Ron Walter.

Olivier Meslay
Felda and Dena Hardymon Director

ACKNOWLEDGMENTS

This publication seeks to add, in a modest way, to the vast corpus of Picasso literature by addressing the issue of his collaborations with others. The same is true for any book, large or small: collaboration is essential. This book was the product of an intense, if relatively short, period of gestation for four additional members of the Clark staff. Anne Roecklein led the publications team with grace and determination, and Ashton Fancy doggedly tracked down numerous images and kept us to our deadlines. Williams College graduate intern Michael Hartman assisted us with research, combing countless books for accurate citations. Genevieve Hulley was the true champion of the rest of the book and the exhibition, creating (and re-creating) the checklist, helping to secure photography from private collectors, and keeping a positive attitude along the way. Roy Brooks of Fold Four created an elegant design, and Sharon Herson copyedited the book with an expert eye.

Many institutions and individuals have lent generously to this exhibition. I am grateful especially to Starr Figura at the Museum of Modern Art; Jennifer Farrell at the Metropolitan Museum of Art; Danielle Canter, Shelley Langdale, and Innis Shoemaker at the Philadelphia Museum of Art; and Helen Burnham and Patrick Murphy at the Museum of Fine Arts, Boston, for working with the Clark on many inquiries, visits, and requests for information. Catherine Woodard and Nelson Blitz, Jr. welcomed me to their home and have lent not only great works of art but their enthusiasm to this project. John Szoke and his associate Chuck Loesner at the John Szoke Gallery likewise supported this exhibition with expertise and loans. John was particularly munificent with his time and helped me on many occasions to craft the checklist. Lastly, I am grateful to the private collectors who wish to remain anonymous.

Several scholars offered their time and expertise to this book and the creation of the checklist. Deborah Wye and Mark Pascale worked with me to ensure the inclusion of a broad range of works. Anne Umland offered sage advice. Jenny Anger commented on an early draft of my essay, and Diana Widmaier-Picasso answered specific questions. Anne-Françoise Gavanon helped us to sort out the complex proof printings of the reduction linocuts *Luncheon on the Grass*. Most importantly, my coauthor Marilyn McCully added great depth to this project not only with her superb text but also with her vast knowledge of the artist. Marilyn saved me from many mistakes and inaccuracies and was gracious with her welcome comments on my essay.

Finally I am grateful to our director, Olivier Meslay, and the curatorial staff at the Clark, especially Mattie Kelley, Kathleen Morris, and Teresa O'Toole for being such kind and patient colleagues. I save the best for last and thank my children, Cora and Liam, for tolerating my heightened stress levels.

Jay A. Clarke

NOTES TO THE READER

Catalogues Raisonnés and Abbreviations

In the event that a particular publication (generally a catalogue raisonné) has become a standard reference for the artist, works are listed with the corresponding reference number. All efforts have been made to indicate state and/or edition. The specific numbering systems are explained in Baer, Mourlot, and Zervos (see below for full bibliographic information). Abbreviations for each catalogue raisonné are as follows:

Baer

Geiser, Bernhard, rev. Brigitte Baer. *Picasso peintre-graveur.* Vols. 1 and 2. Bern: Éditions Kornfeld, 1990–92.

Baer, Brigitte. *Picasso peintre-graveur.* Vols. 3–7 and *Addendum.* Extending the 2-volume work of Bernhard Geiser. Bern: Éditions Kornfeld, 1986–96.

Mourlot

Mourlot, Fernand. *Picasso: The Lithographic Work.* Vol. 1, *1919–1949,* and Vol. 2, *1949–1969.* Revised 2009 by The Picasso Project. San Francisco: Alan Wofsy Fine Arts, 2009.

Zervos

Zervos, Christian. *Pablo Picasso, Catalogue of Works, 1895–1972.* 33 vols. Paris: Éditions "Cahiers d'art," 1932–1978.

Titles

When Picasso's title is not inscribed on the work, we have deferred to the title given in the catalogue raisonné. We have translated titles into English.

Inscriptions

Inscriptions have been transcribed when legible and are given in italics. The media and locations of the inscriptions are noted. All inscriptions are for recto; we do not make note of inscriptions on the verso. The following abbreviations have been used for inscriptions:

l.l. = lower left
l.r. = lower right
l.c. = lower center
u.l. = upper left
u.r. = upper right

Dimensions

Measurements are given in inches and centimeters, with height preceding width.

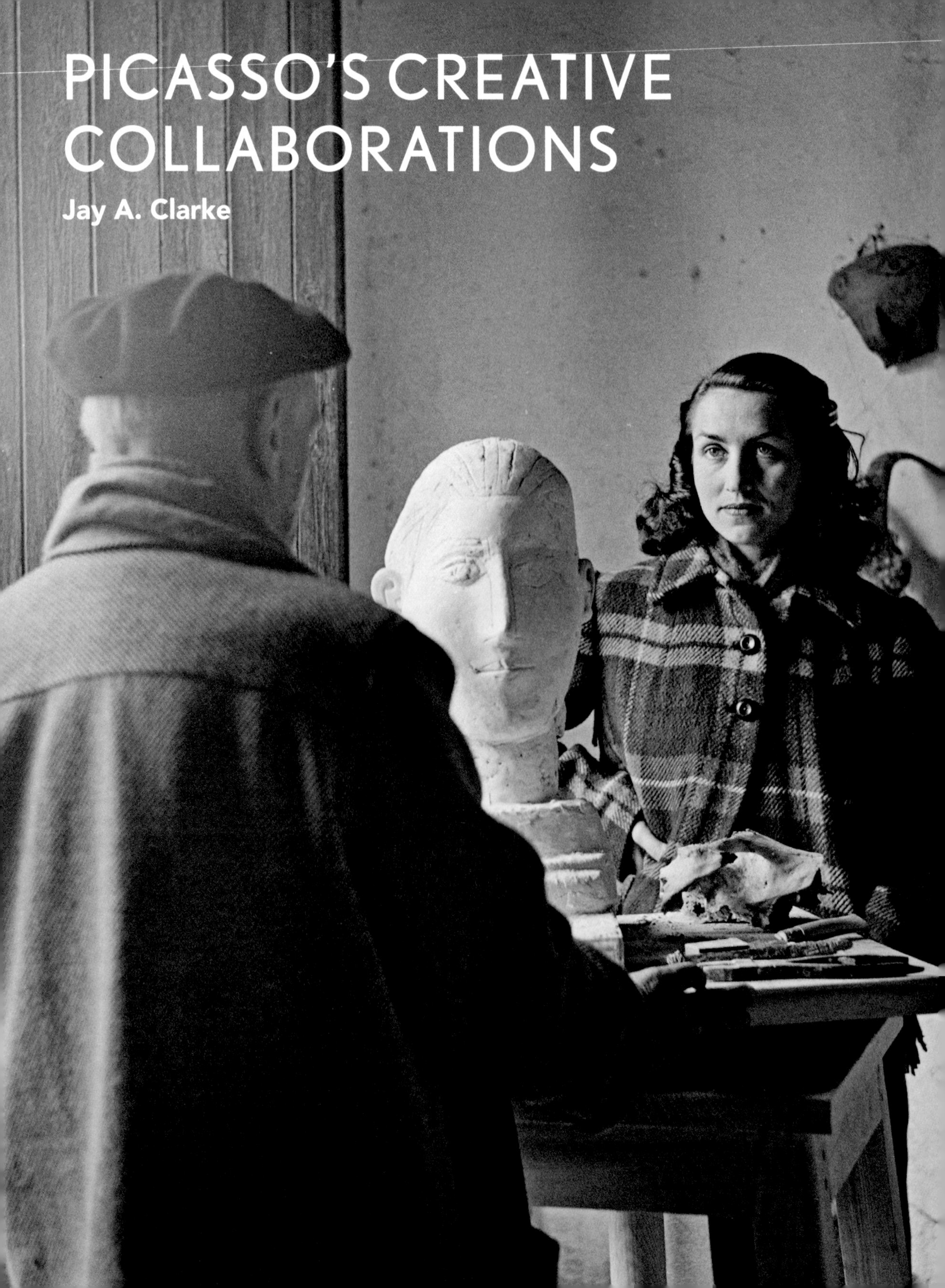

PICASSO'S CREATIVE
COLLABORATIONS

Jay A. Clarke

Picasso's art and life have been chronicled as fecund, both in the quantity and variety of art he made and in the number of women he held in his orbit. Regarded as the ultimate artist-genius, there is no corner of his biography or artistic production that has been left unexamined. Perhaps more than any artist of his era—with the possible exception of Vincent van Gogh (1853–1890)—Picasso's art has been considered homologous with his life. Each affair, each marriage, each stylistic shift, each change in residence has been dissected to arrive at a suitable "explanation" or symbolic meaning behind a particular painting, sculpture, ceramic vessel, print, or drawing. Picasso lived a long life, working for over seven decades as a professional artist, and his career has been broken into bits and pieces according to chronology, lover, aesthetic movement, and political regime as means to better understand his immense production. As the artist himself said in 1932: "The body of work one creates is a form of diary,"[1] and it is often this diaristic approach that critics, art historians, and biographers have used to "explain" his art.[2]

Yet the artist's oeuvre is rarely considered from the perspective of creative collaboration. More often than not, he is the maestro, the conductor of his universe. Despite his notoriously controlling personality, Picasso did not create in a vacuum. For example, only recently have scholars begun to investigate the printers who pulled the images off his copper plates, zinc plates, lithographic stones, and linoleum blocks.[3] This subject is lucidly addressed in Marilyn McCully's essay that follows. Once the issue of Picasso's collaboration with printers comes into focus, however, our field of inquiry can expand. What about the foundries that cast his bronzes, the publishers who commissioned and sold his prints and bronzes, and the ceramicists who threw the pots he later completed? And how did the many muses in his life impact his production? Certainly they served to inspire and, by turns, revile Picasso, but what part did they play in the atmosphere of the studio or in the homes they shared? A good deal is known about his collaboration with Georges Braque (1882–1963) during the period when they co-invented Cubism, but theirs was a relationship of equals, not one of "master" and "artisan" or artist and muse. It is the latter I will address in this essay, as a way to investigate how Picasso's creative collaborations fueled and strengthened his art.

The term *collaboration*, in 2017, is used in a democratizing way. It is unlikely that the artist himself thought of this division of labor as collaborative per se; he was the artist, and they were the artisans or day laborers who worked for him or the wives and partners who loved him. In the twenty-first century we talk of "teams" and "teaming," and I do not suggest this was in any way the kind of relationship Picasso had with his printers or muses.[4] But allowing them to have a voice—an agency, as it were—in the creative process opens up a field of discursive interpretation that can be productive as we unpack the notion of the artist-god creator. Picasso was no doubt an artistic genius; that is not at issue. But it is worthwhile to demonstrate how his "genius" was nurtured and encouraged through the expertise of others, people whose roles have been insufficiently questioned or acknowledged.

Picasso was certainly an agent in these perceptions. His powerful *Self-Portrait* of late 1901 (cat. no. 1) epitomizes this sense of isolation. Here we see Picasso directly meeting our gaze, his dark eyes surrounded by black paint and his hair a helmet atop a thinned face. Besides the white of his pale face, the orange-tinged moustache and beard, and the pink lips, the rest of the painting is an essay in blue from his voluminous jacket to the amorphously striated background. The artist's so-called Blue Period, from 1901 to 1904, was marked by such images of despair, loneliness, and poverty.

Picasso's first large-scale print, *The Frugal Repast* (cat. no. 2), as McCully details in her essay, was printed by Eugène Delâtre (1864–1938), as was the entire series of fifteen to which it later belonged, *The Suite of Saltimbanques* (*Circus Performers*). Delâtre printed them in a small edition in 1905, and it was not until 1911 that the dealer Ambroise Vollard (1867–1939) bought the plates and had them printed in a larger edition of 279 impressions on different papers by Louis Fort (active c. 1927). The differences in the two printings and the results of the two printers are quite telling. Eugène Delâtre, son of the esteemed printer Auguste Delâtre, was an artist in his own right and was instrumental in encouraging his friends, such as Edgar Chahine (1874–1947) and Manuel Robbe (1872–1936), to work in color etching. He advertised his services both to print intaglio plates for artists and to offer them private instruction.[5] While works like *Woman with a Parasol* (fig. 1) exemplify his abilities as a colorist and printer, his subject matter was rather derivative.

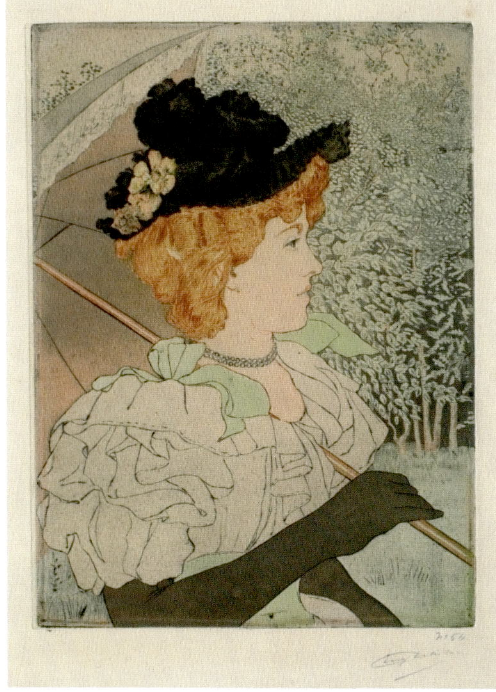

Fig. 1

Picasso complained that Delâtre would not allow him in the
printer's atelier. It seems the printer preferred to add his own
creative touches to the prints, interpreting them for himself,
something Camille Pissarro had complained about a decade
before, arguing that "awful" Delâtre "overdoes it."[6] As is evident
in the Clark's impression of *The Frugal Repast*, Delâtre left inky
areas of tone on the plate, which gave texture and depth to the
print (fig. 2). This can be seen in the tablecloth and the still-life
that sits upon it. By contrast, the impressions pulled by Fort after
the plate was steel-faced (fig. 3) are even and thinly inked, leaving
very little volume to the forms. The process of steel-facing—
when a thin coating of steel covers the copper plate to allow for
numerous impressions to be printed—changes the surface of
the plate, allowing for less detail and nuance. As well, the inking
by Fort was markedly dry and uniform. Picasso could not control
the early printings of *The Frugal Repast* and *Salomé* (cat. no. 3),
and their artistry was, in part, due to the abilities of another.
With Fort, Vollard's main printer, he could give instruction and
not be challenged.

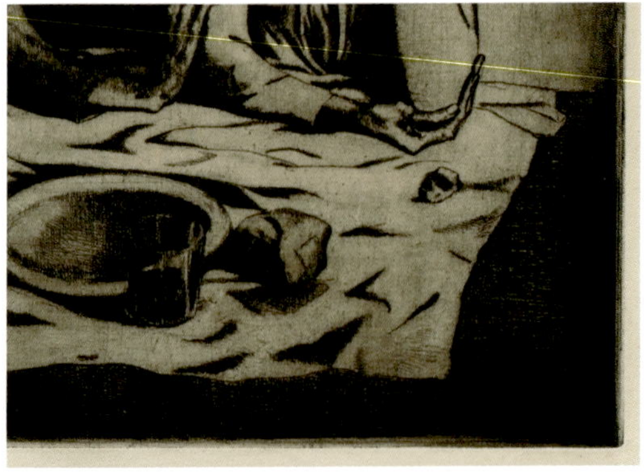

Fig. 2

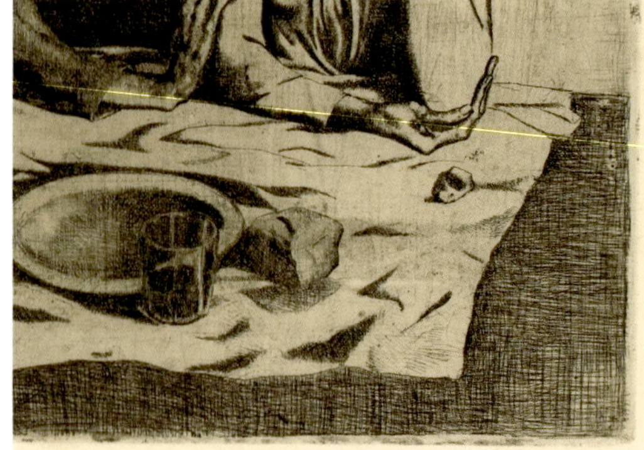

Fig. 3

Two years later, Picasso created the rough-hewn woodcut *Bust of a Young Woman* (cat. no. 4), which depicts Fernande Olivier (1881–1966), his lover from 1904 to 1912. Far less explored than many of his prints, this woodcut was never published, and it was, unusually, printed by the artist himself in a small edition of fifteen in 1933. This was the year Olivier published her memoir *Picasso and His Friends*, and it is possible the event prompted the artist to reprint the block.[7] Picasso and Olivier traveled to Gósol, in the Spanish Pyrenees, during the summer of 1906. The artist was encouraged to sculpt in wood and created the haunting figural piece *Bust of a Woman (Fernande*; also known as *Bois de Gósol)* (fig. 4). This depicts Fernande emerging from a block of wood, supposedly carved with a pocket knife.[8] The elegant Olivier, whom we see in figure 5, dressed in a Spanish costume, has been transformed into a simplified, one could say "primitive," depiction that many have associated with Paul Gauguin's (1848–1903) woodcuts of the 1890s.[9] Olivier, who began her career as a professional model for numerous artists, including Ricard Canals (1876–1931) and Joaquim Sunyer Miró (1874–1956), became Picasso's first muse. She appeared in countless works during this crucial moment as Picasso exploded onto the world stage in a period that marked his initial experimentations with Cubism.

Picasso's aforementioned collaboration with Braque in the development of the Cubist idiom has been extensively documented.[10]

Fig. 2
Pablo Picasso (Spanish, 1881–1973), *The Frugal Repast* (detail), 1904. Etching on paper, plate: 18 1/8 × 14 7/8 in. (46.1 × 37.8 cm); sheet: 20 15/16 × 17 7/16 in. (53.2 × 44.3 cm). Clark Art Institute, 1962.89

Fig. 3
Pablo Picasso, *The Frugal Repast* (detail), from *The Suite of Saltimbanques*, 1904, printed and published 1913. Etching on zinc in black on cream wove paper, image/plate 18 7/8 × 15 in. (48 × 38 cm); sheet 25 3/4 × 20 in. (65.5 × 50.8 cm). Art Institute of Chicago, Gift of Walter S. Brewster, 1948.326

Clarke

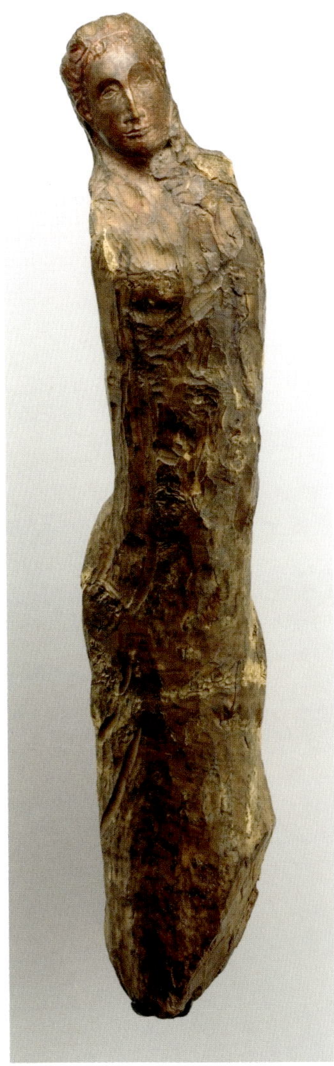

Fig. 4

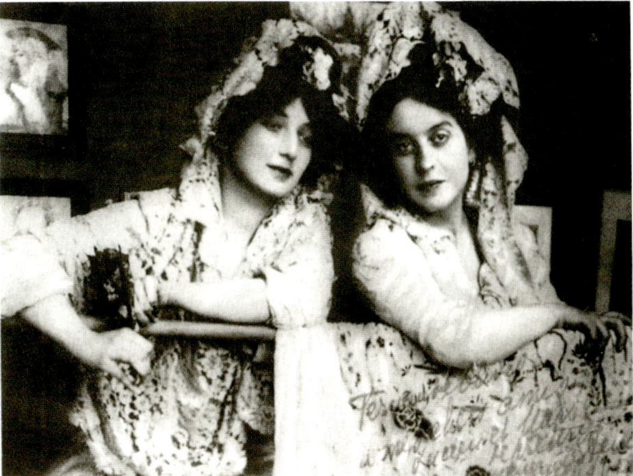

Fig. 5

During the years 1910–12, the artists worked together to invent a radical new style in which form and space were exploded and then reconstructed. Living in Montmartre and working in constant dialogue with one another to explore this new style, the two took to wearing mechanics' outfits and describing their work in the studio as "manual labor."[11] Their synergistic approach is evinced in the fact that, for a time, the two eschewed signing their works, a practice that the prominent dealer Daniel-Henry Kahnweiler (1884–1979) described as "a deliberate gesture towards *impersonal* authorship."[12] This elision of signature, a practice overturned once their collaboration became less intense around 1912, marks a moment of true self-abnegation when Picasso subsumed his own ego for the sake of creative partnership. Braque described the two as "roped together like mountain climbers," signifying a level of trust and unification that we will see repeated in Picasso's creative collaborations with printers and muses, but perhaps never again with such a level of perceived equality.[13]

Picasso created a handful of Cubist prints during this period, the most important being *Still-Life with Bottle of Marc* (cat. no. 5). The iconography has been investigated at length, from the brandy called Marc that gave the print its title to the presence of playing cards at the bottom half of the print with the ace of hearts said to signify Picasso's new lover, Eva Gouel.[14] A fact that is less remarked upon is that Kahnweiler commissioned the print.[15]

Fig. 4
Pablo Picasso, *Bust of a Woman (Fernande)/Bois de Gósol*, summer 1906. Wood sculpture with traces of polychromy (front view), 30⅜ × 6¾ × 5⅞ in. (77 × 17 × 15 cm). Musée national Picasso-Paris, inv. MP233

Fig. 5
Fernande and Benedetta in Spanish costume in Canals' studio, 1904.

Kahnweiler (fig. 6), whom Picasso depicted in a Cubist portrait
of 1910, was among the most important supporters of Cubism
in its infancy, giving Braque his first exhibition and promoting
Picasso as well, prompting the artist to remark: "What would
have become of us if Kahnweiler had not had a good business
sense?"[16] Indeed, *Still-Life with Bottle of Marc*, among Picasso's
first editioned single-sheet prints, was commissioned by Kahnweiler
probably as a way to market the artist more widely through
the dissemination of prints. For many young artists starting their
careers in Paris at this time, printmaking was often a way for
dealers to promote and artists to gain needed income.

Picasso's experimentations with Cubism shifted during the war
years, and he found a new fascination: costume and theater design.
It was through the theater that he met his first wife, the Russian
dancer Olga Khokhlova (1891–1955; fig. 7).[17] Khokhlova was in
the corps of Sergei Diaghilev's (1872–1929) highly respected Ballets
Russes, but she chose to leave the corps shortly before she and
Picasso married in 1918. They moved to a fashionable neighbor-
hood in Paris and began to entertain and mix with the elite, a shift
from Picasso's earlier bohemian circles. Picasso's upward mobility
in both the art market and the elegant, sophisticated lifestyle with
Khokhlova began to appear in his art. The drypoint *Portrait of Olga
in a Fur Collar* (cat. no. 6) depicts his wife dressed in the height
of fashion, serenely turned to the side.

Among the most iconic of muses in Picasso's career was Marie-
Thérèse Walter (1909–1977; fig. 8), whether as an actual figure
in his art or as a projected motif. The beginning of the end
for Picasso and Khokhlova occurred in 1927 when the artist met
Walter, supposedly on a Paris street.[18] Walter would become
both an erotic and a visual preoccupation for Picasso during an
immensely productive time in his life, thereby cementing her
"place" in his pantheon of lovers. Her youth and classical beauty
are evident in a lithograph of the following year, *Visage (Face
of Marie-Thérèse*; cat. no. 7), which was created as a frontispiece
for a monograph on the artist by the Parisian collector and critic
André Level but was also issued separately in an edition of one
hundred on different papers.[19] When the two met, Walter was
seventeen to Picasso's forty. Her physical presence as his lover
is certainly different from the inventive realm she unleashed
for the artist—a realm that was, significantly, secret. Her identity

Fig. 6
Pablo Picasso, *Daniel-Henry Kahnweiler*, autumn 1910. Oil on canvas, 39 9/16 × 28 9/16 in. (100.4 × 72.4 cm). Art Institute of Chicago, Gift of Mrs. Gilbert W. Chapman in memory of Charles B. Goodspeed, 1948.561

Fig. 7
Olga Khokhlova in costume for the Shéhérazade ballet, 1916. Photograph, 4 1/2 × 3 in. (11.5 × 7.5 cm)

Fig. 8
Marie-Thérèse Walter with her dog Dolly (at Cité d'Alfort, Maisons-Alfort), c. 1930.

Clarke

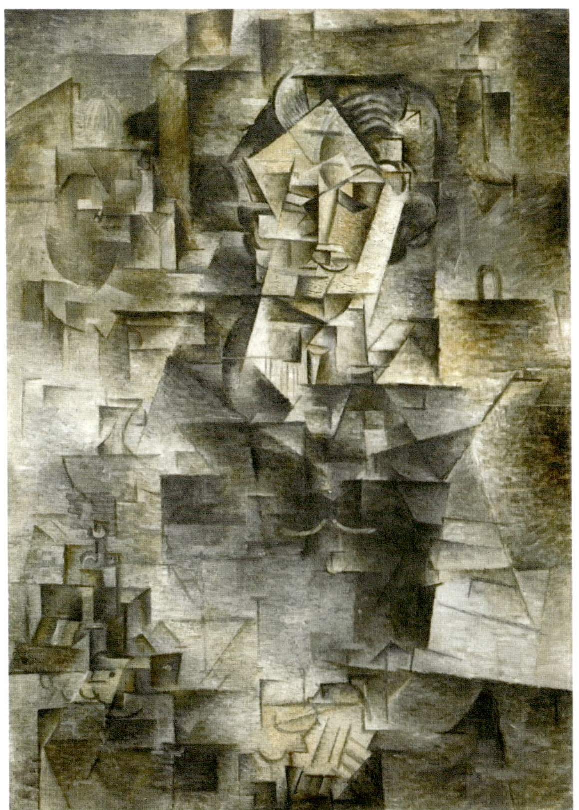

Fig. 6

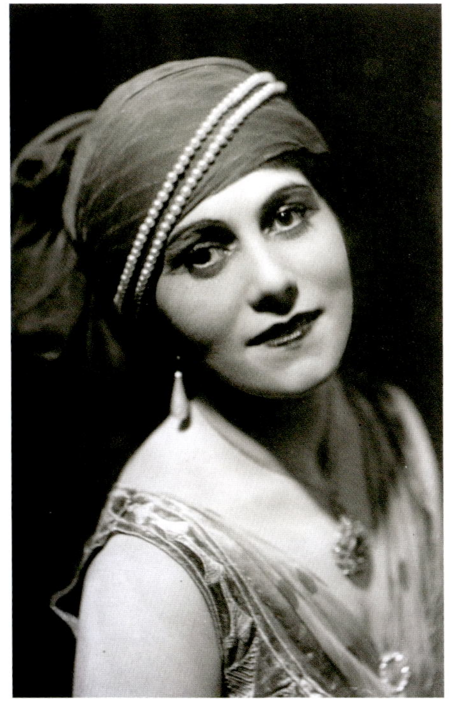

Fig. 7

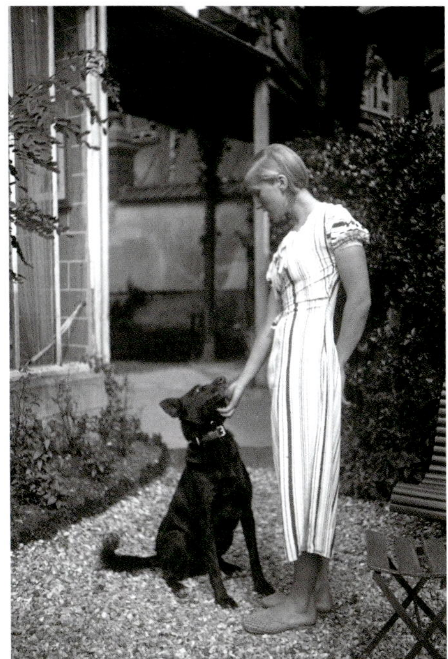

Fig. 8

remained supposedly unknown to his wife Khokhlova until the birth of Walter and Picasso's child Maya in 1935 and to the world at large until 1964 when a revealing book was published by Picasso's then-ex-lover Françoise Gilot (b. 1921).[20]

Walter's numerous manifestations in Picasso's prints of the 1930s are less portrait-like than *Visage (Face of Marie-Thérèse)*. Instead, her image appears frequently as a thematic inspiration, her profile immediately recognizable. As is the case throughout his career, many of the prints from this period have been described as autobiographical. For example, in the *Large Bullfight, with Female Bullfighter* (cat. no. 9), Walter has been associated with the female toreador, Picasso with the bull, and Khokhlova with the enraged horse who throws the mistress and lances the artist. Yet the representations of Walter, as lover (cat. no. 12), child (cat. nos. 10 and 11), statue (cat. no. 8), and as wounded bullfighter (cat. no. 11), move beyond biography and into the realm of myth and allegory. From 1930 to 1937, Picasso created *The Vollard Suite*, named after the dealer Vollard, who commissioned the series. In this suite of one hundred prints, male-oriented Minotaurs, fauns, and bulls enact violent and/or sexual fantasies with the objects of their desire, female-oriented creatures or humans. The series also contains more serene images of an artist in his studio, creating sculpture. In *Two Clothed Models* (cat. no. 8), we see the features of Marie-Thérèse as both model and sculpture, here rendered in a pure, neo-classically etched line.

These prints raise the issue of the muse as both a creative impetus and an object of rage. Picasso was a man who preferred his women to be subjugated, and he wished to remain in control. As his partner Françoise Gilot, who left him in 1953, said to a reporter in 2011: "[I] am the only woman who left Picasso, the only one who did not sacrifice herself to the sacred monster."[21] The muse as depicted in *The Vollard Suite* is mostly a passive object of desire. In *Faun Unveiling a Sleeping Girl* (cat. no. 12), the voluptuous woman is naked and vulnerable with her slumbering form available for all to see and for the faun to touch. In the biographical reading, Picasso is the sexually aroused faun and Marie-Thérèse is the young nude woman placed under a vulva-shaped tent, passive and open to his advances. In *Blind Minotaur* (cat. no. 10), the stand-in for Picasso (if we choose to see him that way), the terrifyingly vulnerable Minotaur, is being led by a little girl with the face of Marie-Thérèse. Either way, as aggressor or dependent, the mythological creature needs the woman, for appetite or for survival.

Although the Picasso literature tends to interpret his various muses as passive, objectified, even abused, the fact is that he needed them. Picasso needed his wives, partners, and mistresses as inspiration for his art. He also wanted them to help him keep his home and create a family life. Yes, he had secretaries like his friend Jaime Sabartés (1881–1968) to help him keep his creative output and financial affairs in order, but Picasso seemed unable or unwilling to function without a life partner, regardless of how he treated them. Why not look at their essential role in his life as one of collaboration instead of as just master/servant? Regardless of whether he was a masochist and a tormenter, a cheater and an abuser, Walter, and later Jacqueline Roque (1927–1986), remained devoted to Picasso their entire lives; they needed him as much as he needed them, albeit in different ways. This combination of victim and agent may seem antithetical, but human relations are complex.

Picasso's seemingly dichotomous treatment of his lovers as adored and then despised or replaced can be summed up in a quote by him as remembered by Gilot: "Every time I change wives I should burn the last one. That way I'd be rid of them. They wouldn't be around now to complicate my existence. Maybe, that would bring back my youth, too. You kill the woman and you wipe out the past she represents."[22] This remark is telling in that Picasso expresses the need to purge his past the moment the relationship comes to an end in order to reclaim his youth and avoid "complications" or interruptions to his life. In these words, Picasso described women only as they impacted his life, not how he impacted theirs. In another telling quote, the artist argued: "There are only two types of women: goddesses and doormats."[23] While they often began as goddesses, it seems, they often ended up as doormats.

Soon after Walter gave birth to their daughter Maya, and while still married to but separated from Khokhlova, Picasso began a relationship with the Surrealist photographer Dora Maar (1907–1997; fig. 9). As was his pattern, this new muse began to appear frequently in his work; for example, in the striking *Portrait of Dora Maar* of 1937 (cat. no. 13). Here we see the sitter in a hieratic pose, her Cubist-rendered face seen in three-quarter view. Her

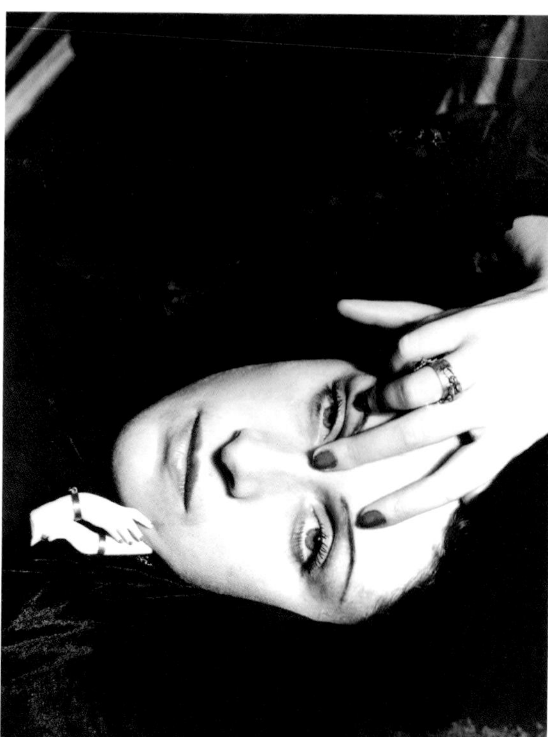

Fig. 9

scissor-like hands are crowned with pointed red fingernails, and her top comprises vibrant colors, decorated with blue and black nail-like objects that taper toward her waist. These sharp components, when coupled with the claustrophobic, enclosed space of Maar's room, provide a sense of brittle unease.

The physiological elements of sharp fingernails and coiffed black hair reappear in one of Picasso's most powerful graphic statements, *The Weeping Woman, I* (cat nos. 14, 15). A ferocious image of grief, at once compelling and frightening, the print is one of the largest created in the wake of his iconic *Guernica* (fig. 20). On April 26, 1937, the forces of General Francisco Franco (1892–1975) bombed the undefended town of Guernica in the Basque region of northern Spain. Picasso's *Guernica* expressed the horrors of war and the carnage endured by the helpless civilians, victims of fascism. After completing *Guernica*, Picasso continued to be drawn to the subject of grief, and he undertook a series of drawings, paintings, and prints depicting the subject of the "weeping woman."[24] In the

Clarke

large-scale print, as in the two smaller manifestations of the subject—*The Weeping Woman, III* (cat. no. 16) and *The Weeping Woman, IV* (cat. no. 17)—the figure is distorted in a silent shriek of pain. The woman, who resembles Dora Maar, raises a scissor-like hand to wipe away the spiked tears that incise the overlapping planes of her contorted face.

The Weeping Woman, I, III, and *IV*, and the subsequent *Woman with Tambourine* (cat. no. 18), were, in part, carried off with the immense talent of Picasso's printer Roger Lacourière (1892–1966). Lacourière was, like Delâtre, an artist himself but, unlike Delâtre, considered himself an "artisan" in the printing studio with Picasso and was therefore possibly perceived as less of a threat. As Brigitte Baer has argued, the Lacourière shop had countless presses, workers, and all the tools necessary for Picasso to invent at will, as well as an immense amount of experience on which to draw. The monumental *Weeping Woman, I* in its third (cat. no. 14) and final, seventh (cat. no. 15) state was printed in small editions of fifteen impressions each and published by the artist himself. The third state depicts the woman in fairly simple lines of etching and drypoint, with a spare use of aquatint and plate tone for depth. By contrast, the final state includes far more work on the plate, scoring the hair, eyes, nails, teeth, and face to create a haunting and disturbing yet arresting face of despair. Picasso's ability to create beauty out of ostensible ugliness in this print acts simultaneously to attract and repel.[25]

Shortly before Picasso became involved in politics, creating works for anti-war causes, such as a *The Dove* (cat. no. 21) for the First World Peace Conference in 1949 (fig. 21), his relationship with Maar was deteriorating and another muse soon took her place. He met the twenty-one-year-old painter Gilot in 1943, a relationship that was later detailed in her aforementioned literary portrayal of Picasso. The pair had two children, Claude and Paloma (fig. 10), and Gilot later remarked how Picasso spent "hours" painting and drawing them.[26] Their births prompted many tender and playful works. As Werner Spies has convincingly argued, Picasso's representations of his own offspring show stylistic restraint, and, in them, the artist was concerned with calm portrayal rather than extreme distortion or experimentation.[27] The large-scale lithograph *Paloma and Her Doll on Black Background* (cat. no. 24) attests to the influence his children had on his work in terms of

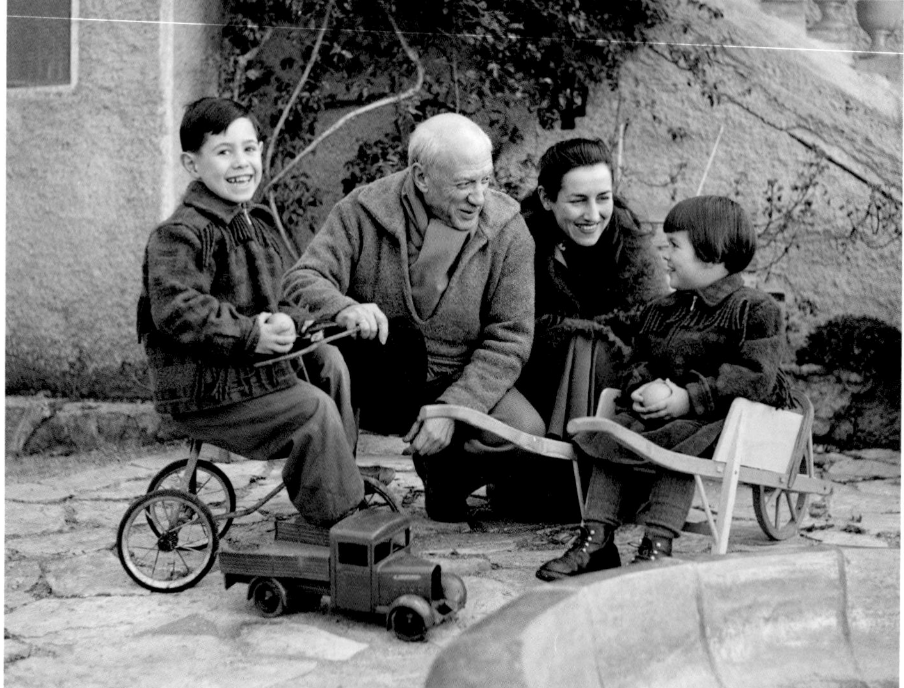

Fig. 10

inspiration and subject matter. Here we see Paloma's round, faceted face accentuated by a page-boy haircut, sweetly staring out at the viewer while holding a doll whose face is similarly rendered in depth. The strength of the lithographic crayon in this work is, technically speaking, the polar opposite of *The Dove*, which was created by the painterly application of tusche wash with a brush whereas *Paloma* is primarily linear, made by drawing with a lithographic crayon and then scraping away for the light portions of her face and that of the doll.

As McCully details in her text, in his various approaches to print-making, Picasso pushed every medium to its limits. One print of 1953 exemplifies Picasso's co-option of photography in printmak-ing, a rather unusual practice for him.[28] During this period, while working with the lithographic printers at the Mourlot Frères shop, directed by Fernand Mourlot (1895–1988), Picasso often used chemically prepared zinc plates that could create lithographs, sometimes called zincographs. Cheaper and more portable than heavy lithographic stones, the zincograph came into wider use

Clarke

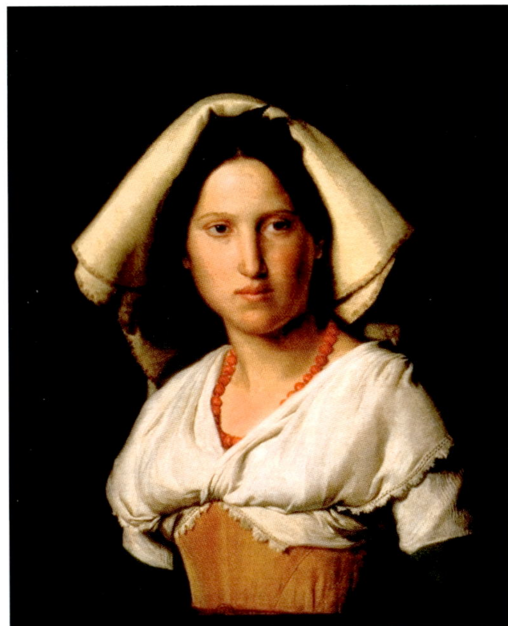

Fig. 11

in Europe in the 1890s.[29] In 1953, during a tumultuous period
with Gilot, Picasso went to Paris to work with Mourlot and found
a discarded zinc plate in his atelier, upon which a photograph
had been transferred of a painting by Victor Orsel (1795–1850),
Portrait of Vittoria Caldoni, or *The Young Italian* (fig. 11). The plate
had been discarded to be ground down and reused, but Picasso
chose to rework it (cat. no. 25). He scratched into the plate a
man playing castanets, a flute-playing faun, and a nude woman;
and he changed the features of the main figure, who, some have
argued, then resembled his new love interest Jacqueline Roque,
to whom we will return.[30]

Two of Picasso's last printed depictions of Gilot—*Woman at the
Window* (cat. no. 23) and *The Egyptian Woman* (cat. no. 26)—
were large-scale *tours de force*, prints made with Lacourière using
a newly invented process known as sugar-lift aquatint. Standard
aquatint, which Picasso used in *Faun Unveiling a Sleeping Faun*
and *The Weeping Woman, I*, is created by fusing a dusty resin
onto a copper plate by heating the plate and then immersing it

in an acid bath. The acid eats away at the uneven particles of resin and, when inked and printed, the aquatint creates a wash-like tone. However, the sugar-lift process suited Picasso because with it, tonal areas could be directly painted on a plate. A sugary syrup is mixed with ink, and this liquid substance is painted on a plate coated with resin. Once dry, the plate is then coated with varnish and placed in a shallow bath of water. The water causes the sugar-ink combination to "lift off" the plate (hence the term "sugar-lift"), leaving the area that has been drawn bare. When placed in an acid bath, the plate is then bitten precisely where the drawing was created (fig. 12).[31] The immediacy of this process appealed to the impatient Picasso, who did not like to wait for printers to do the intermediary work while he awaited the results.[32]

Woman at the Window (cat. no. 23) depicts Gilot the year before she left Picasso with her children in tow, and evinces an interesting, if probably accidental, instance of collaboration. Gilot is depicted in a partly Cubist vein with her chest, hair, and face broken into facets and her hands presented as large and clumsy. She presses her hands and face against the window as if wishing to escape her confinement in an abusive relationship with Picasso. At the upper right, cursive lettering is barely visible coming down diagonally as if on a shaft of light (fig. 13); it reads "Lacourière." The signature is backwards as would be the case if the printer had signed in a regular orientation, as the printing would reverse it. The printer would have known of this reversal, and it is possible he retained it so as to keep the signature subtle. While the presence of printers' signatures was not unknown at the turn of the twentieth century, it was a highly unusual inclusion in the 1950s.[33] It has been suggest-ed that the signature was left on the plate by someone who was going to deliver it to the printer, but if it was accidental, then why did both artist and printer leave it there for the entire edition to be printed? One can surmise that as Picasso's relationship with Gilot began to strain, another creative collaborator, Lacourière, was a comforting and distracting interlocutor.

The final muse in Picasso's life was his second wife and companion of twenty years, Jacqueline Roque. He met Roque in the summer of 1952 while she was working at the Madoura pottery works, around the time that his relationship with Gilot was deteriorating. While some have described Roque as having a monster-like possessive-ness of Picasso, combined with a doormat-like submissiveness,

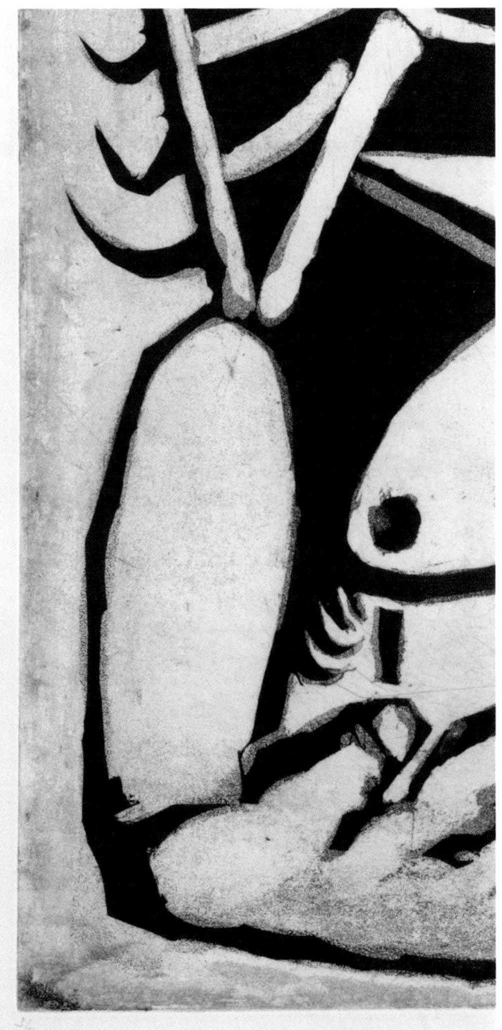

Fig. 13

Fig. 12

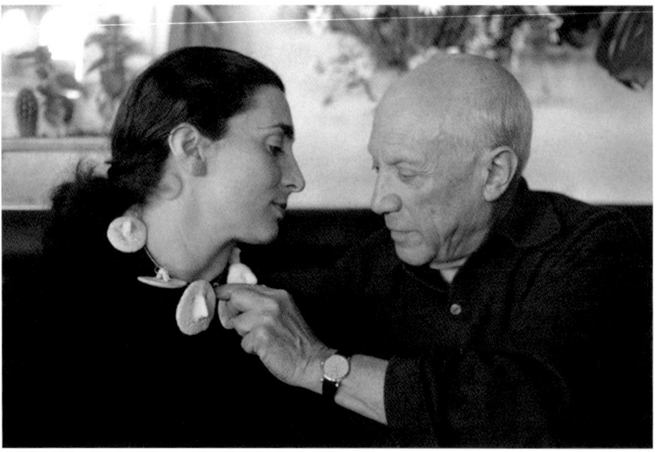

Fig. 14
David Douglas Duncan (American, b. 1916), *Pablo Picasso adjusting a necklace he made for Jacqueline Roque*, c. 1957. Photograph

Fig. 15
Roberto Otero (Argentine, 1931–2004), *Picasso showing his works in a secret room. In the back on the right "Nude Woman" (1904), on the left "Bust of a Woman" (1941).* Gelatin silver suspension, 7 ⅞ × 11 ¾ in. (19.9 × 29.7 cm)

others have noted their loving relationship.[34] Regardless, Roque was a constant presence in his life and in his artistic production (fig. 14).[35] Her dark hair, almond-shaped eyes, and aquiline nose are seen in the grisaille painting *Jacqueline Knitting* of 1954 (cat. no. 27), which reveals her Mediterranean beauty. Here we see Jacqueline sewing, with her hands, body, hair, and knitting needles and thread broken into crystalline forms. Her large hooded eye, high cheekbone, and nose are rendered naturalistically. Numerous *pentimenti* are visible next to her face and hands where the artist changed his mind on several occasions. In figure 15, we can see Picasso holding up and admiring the painting in his studio; this was a work he kept in his possession until his death.

Woman with a Flowered Blouse (cat. no. 29) is an arresting, heavily worked lithograph that Picasso created of Jacqueline over a one-year period from 1957 to 1958. Interestingly, he dates the print within the stone with three different months: December 12, 1957; February 1, 1958; and December 27, 1958. As with many of his late lithographs of Jacqueline, Picasso would date each

Clarke

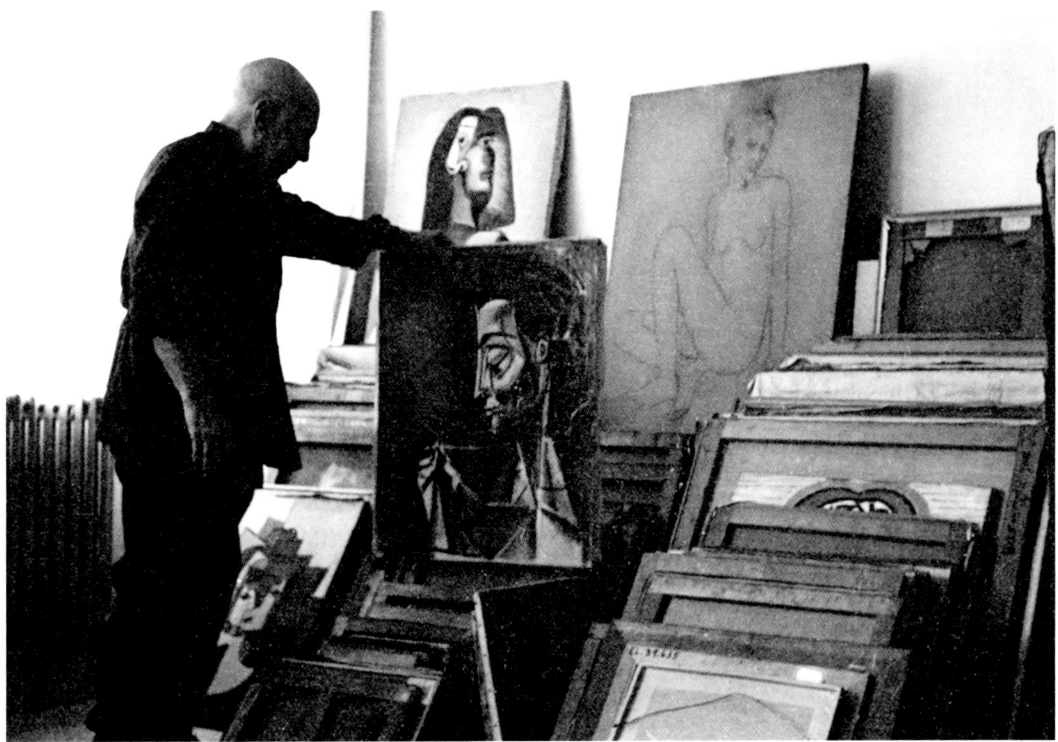

Fig. 15

successive proof as he worked on the zinc plate. The sheet is
made up of tusche wash in the blouse and hair, as well as in the
profile of her face (the first state). In the second state he added
more tusche in the blouse and hair, lithographic crayon in the
background, shading in her face, as well as minor scraping in
the blouse. The final state includes more shading in her face and
the background, with additional scraping in the hair, crossed arms,
and the details of her flower-patterned blouse. As the artist said
to the photographer Brassaï in 1943: "Why do you think I date
everything I do? Because it is not sufficient to know an artist's works.
It is also necessary to know when he made them, why, how, under
what circumstances."[36]

Another lifelong "companion" and muse for Picasso was the
presence of earlier artists, as has been argued in the recent
exhibition *Picasso: Challenging the Past* (2009).[37] His interpretations of Cranach, Rembrandt, Velàzquez, Delacroix, Manet, Degas,
and others are legion, and Picasso frequently took their canvases
as jumping-off points, especially later in his life in the 1950s and

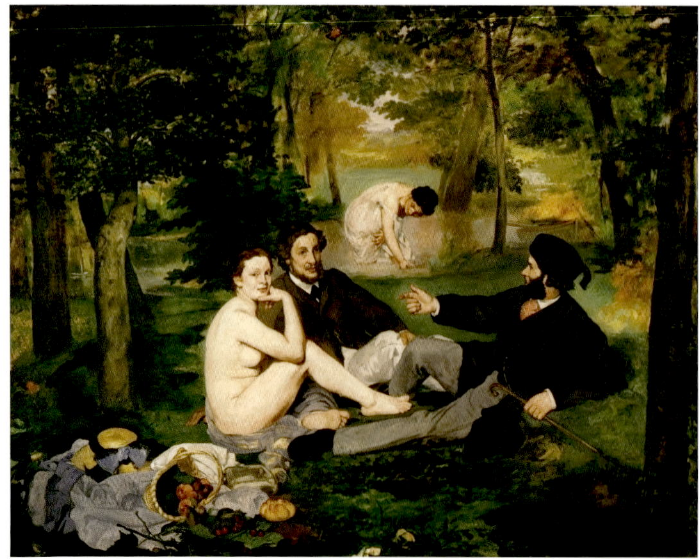

Fig. 16
Édouard Manet (French, 1832–1883),
Déjeuner sur l'herbe (Luncheon on the Grass), 1863. Oil on canvas, 81 ⅞ × 104 ⅛ in. (208 × 264.5 cm). Musée d'Orsay, Paris, inv. RF 1668

1960s. These creative copies, or as Picasso called them, his "dialogues" with artists of the past, were made in all media: paintings, prints, drawings, and sculpture.[38] One such example is the artist's numerous versions after Édouard Manet's (1832–1883) *Luncheon on the Grass* of 1863 (fig. 16). Picasso wrote on the back of an envelope around 1932: "When I see Manet's *Luncheon on the Grass* I tell myself there is pain ahead."[39] Was this "pain" about romantic involvements, artistic challenges, creative jealousy? It is difficult to know, but his many interpretations were in no way copies; rather, they served as homages to Manet and challenges to the eighty-nine-year-old Picasso. After several drawn, painted, and sculpted versions, Picasso created the brightly hued, multicolor linocut (cat. no. 36), one produced in the complex reduction linocut process (see McCully essay). A true collaboration with his printer Hidalgo Arnéra (1922–2007), the numerous unpublished trial proofs (cat. nos. 32–35) included in this exhibition attest to their constant experimentation.

Picasso's creative collaborations, be they with romantic partners or professional printers, fueled his art and imagination in myriad ways.

Clarke

The cult of the individual "artist-genius"—a concept born out of Romanticism—has been associated with Picasso both in his production and in his persona. We can all probably envision Picasso at work or play in our mind's eye—remembering photographs taken by those who documented his art and life. But can we necessarily picture his creative partners? Can many of us name the printers who prepared his lithographic stones or the individuals who threw and then fired his ceramic vessels? The myth and the market around Picasso thrives on his individuality and the cult of his genius as well as on the history of his macho womanizing. But when we give agency to those around him—his supporters, dealers, publishers, children, and lovers—it makes his creative enterprise even more complex and layered. When we give agency to others in his orbit, Picasso's art and production somehow become more alive. In today's global art world, when collaboration and participatory interdependence are the norm, it is refreshing to see how one of the "greats" of the twentieth century was similarly nourished.

NOTES

1. As quoted in Efstratios Tériade, "En causant avec Picasso," *L'Intransigeant*, June 15, 1932, 1.

2. Rosalind Krauss and others have discussed this methodological strain. On the issue of biography, see Rosalind Krauss, "In the Name of Picasso," *October* 16 (Spring 1981): 5–22; and Rosalind Krauss, *The Picasso Papers* (New York: Farrar, Straus, and Giroux, 1998).

3. For example, Brigitte Baer, *Picasso the Printmaker: Graphics from the Marina Picasso Collection* (Dallas: Dallas Museum of Art, 1983); Pat Gilmour, "Picasso and His Printers," *The Print Collector's Newsletter* 18 (July–August 1987): 81–90; Deborah Wye, *A Picasso Portfolio: Prints from the Museum of Modern Art* (New York: Museum of Modern Art, 2010); and Marilyn McCully, *Celebrating the Muse: Women in Picasso's Prints, 1905–1968* (New York: Marlborough Gallery, 2010).

4. On the issue of the muse and the model, see Germaine Greer, "The Role of the Artist's Muse," *Guardian*, June 2, 2008; Karen L. Kleinfelder, *The Artist, His Model, Her Image, His Gaze: Picasso's Pursuit of the Model* (Chicago and London: University of Chicago Press, 1993); Josephine Withers, "Modernism's Muse: Pablo Picasso," *Women's Art Magazine* 56 (January–February 1994): 4–9. Two recent exhibitions have focused on the issue of Picasso and the muse: McCully, *Celebrating the Muse*; and *Picasso and His Muses*, ed. Katharina Beisiegel (Vancouver: Vancouver Art Gallery, 2016). One article that productively considers Picasso's sculptural collaborations is Josephine Withers, "The Artistic Collaboration of Pablo Picasso and Julio González," *Art Journal* 35 (Winter 1975–76): 107–14. For a discussion of collaboration in contemporary art, see Maria Lind, "Complications; On Collaboration, Agency, and Contemporary Art," *Public* 39 (Spring 2009): 52–73.

5. Phillip Denis Cate and Marianne Grivel, *From Pissarro to Picasso: Color Etching in France* (New Brunswick, NJ: Zimmerli Art Museum, 1992), 58–68 and n. 56.

6. *Correspondance de Camille Pissarro*, vol. 4, ed. Janine Bailly-Herzberg (Paris: Presses universitaires de France, 1980), 26. Pissarro went further, calling his color etchings "truly vulgar" (p. 169). For more on Picasso's annoyances with Delâtre, see Brigitte Baer, *Picasso: Peintre-Graveur, Addendum* (Berne: Éditions Kornfeld, 1996), 11–12.

7. Olivier's book *Picasso et ses amis* (Paris: Stock, 1933) was published first in serialized form in French and Belgian newspapers starting in 1930.

8. John Richardson with Marilyn McCully, *A Life of Picasso*, vol. 1 (New York: Random House, 1991), 442–47.

9. McCully, *Celebrating the Muse*, n.p.

10. Eik Kahng, *Picasso and Braque: The Cubist Experiment, 1910–1912* (Santa Barbara: Santa Barbara Museum of Art, 2011); and William Rubin, *Picasso and Braque: Pioneering Cubism* (New York: Museum of Modern Art, 1989).

11. Rubin, *Picasso and Braque*, 19–20.

12. Ibid., 19.

13. As quoted in Dora Vallier, "Bracque, la peinture et nous: Propos de l'artiste recueillis," *Cahiers d'Art* 29 (1954): 14.

14. Baer, *Picasso the Printmaker*, 41.

15. Ibid., 37.

16. Pierre Cabanne, *Pablo Picasso: His Life and Times*, trans. Harold J. Salemson (New York: Morrow, 1977), 139.

17. Olivier Berggruen and Max Hollein, *Picasso and the Theater* (Frankfurt am Main: Schirn Kunsthalle, 2006).

Clarke

18. Michael Fitzgerald, "A Question of Identity," in *Picasso's Marie-Thérèse* (New York: Acquavella Galleries, 2008), 9–29; and Diana Widmaier-Picasso, "Marie-Thérèse Walter and Pablo Picasso: New Insights into a Secret Love," in *Pablo Picasso and Marie-Thérèse Walter: Between Classicism and Surrealism*, ed. Markus Müller (Bielefeld: Kerber, 2004), 27–35.

19. Fernand Mourlot, *Picasso Lithographe* (Paris: André Sauret, 1970), no. 23.

20. Françoise Gilot with Carlton Lake, *Life with Picasso* (New York: McGraw Hill, 1964).

21. As quoted in Janet Hawley, "Pablo was the greatest love of my life. . . . I left before I was destroyed," *Sydney Morning Herald*, July 23, 2011.

22. Gilot, *Life with Picasso*, 349.

23. Ibid., p. 84.

24. For more on this topic, see Judi Freeman, *Picasso and the Weeping Woman: The Years of Marie-Thérèse Walter and Dora Maar* (Los Angeles: Los Angeles County Museum of Art, 1994).

25. For more on the issue of Picasso and ugliness, see J. M. Bernstein, "'The Demand for Ugliness': Picasso's Bodies," in *Art and Aesthetics after Adorno* (Berkeley: University of California Press, 2010), 210–45. My thanks to Mieke Bal for this reference.

26. Gilot, *Life with Picasso*, 256.

27. Werner Spies, *Picasso's World of Children* (Munich: Prestel, 1994), 75–79 and 90–96.

28. For more on Picasso and photography, see Anne Baldassari, *Picasso and Photography: The Dark Mirror* (Houston: Museum of Fine Arts, 1997).

29. For more on the zincograph, see Jay A. Clarke, "Cornelia Paczka-Wagner: Representing the Symbolic Self," *Cantor Arts Center Journal* 7 (2010–11): 77–91.

30. Szoke http://www.johnszoke.com/picasso/land39italienne; accessed January 7, 2017.

31. Bamber Gascoigne, *How to Identify Prints: A Complete Guide to Manual and Mechanical Processes from Woodcut to Inkjet*, 2nd ed. (New York: Thames and Hudson, 2004), 60.

32. Many authors have noted this impatience, including Gilmour, "Picasso and His Printers."

33. One example is the Berlin printer Otto Felsing, who often cosigned the intaglio prints of Käthe Kollwitz, Max Liebermann, and Edvard Munch in the 1890s.

34. For example, David Douglas Duncan, *The Private World of Pablo Picasso* (New York: Ridge Press, 1958). My thanks to Marilyn McCully for this reference.

35. Richard Dorment, "Picasso's Saddest Love," *Daily Telegraph*, January 14, 2004; http://www.telegraph.co.uk/culture/art/3610082/Picassos-saddest-love.html; accessed on January 25, 2017.

36. Brassaï, *Conversations avec Picasso* (Paris: Gallimard, 1964), 123.

37. Elizabeth Cowling, *Picasso: Challenging the Past* (London: National Gallery, 2009).

38. Catherine Soussloff, "Pablo Picasso: Late Works and the Model-Muse," in *Picasso: The Artist and His Muses* (2016), 131. For a discussion of Picasso's inspiration from the old masters, see Markus Müller, "Picasso als Revisor der Museumkunst," in *Picasso: Linolschnitte* (Munich: Hirmer, 2011), 118–32; and Susan Grace Galassi, *Picasso's Variations on the Masters: Confrontations with the Past* (New York: Abrams, 1996).

39. *Picasso's Collected Writings*, ed., Marie-Laure Bernadac and Christine Piot, trans. Carol Volk and Albert Bensoussan (New York: Abbeville Press, 1989), 371.

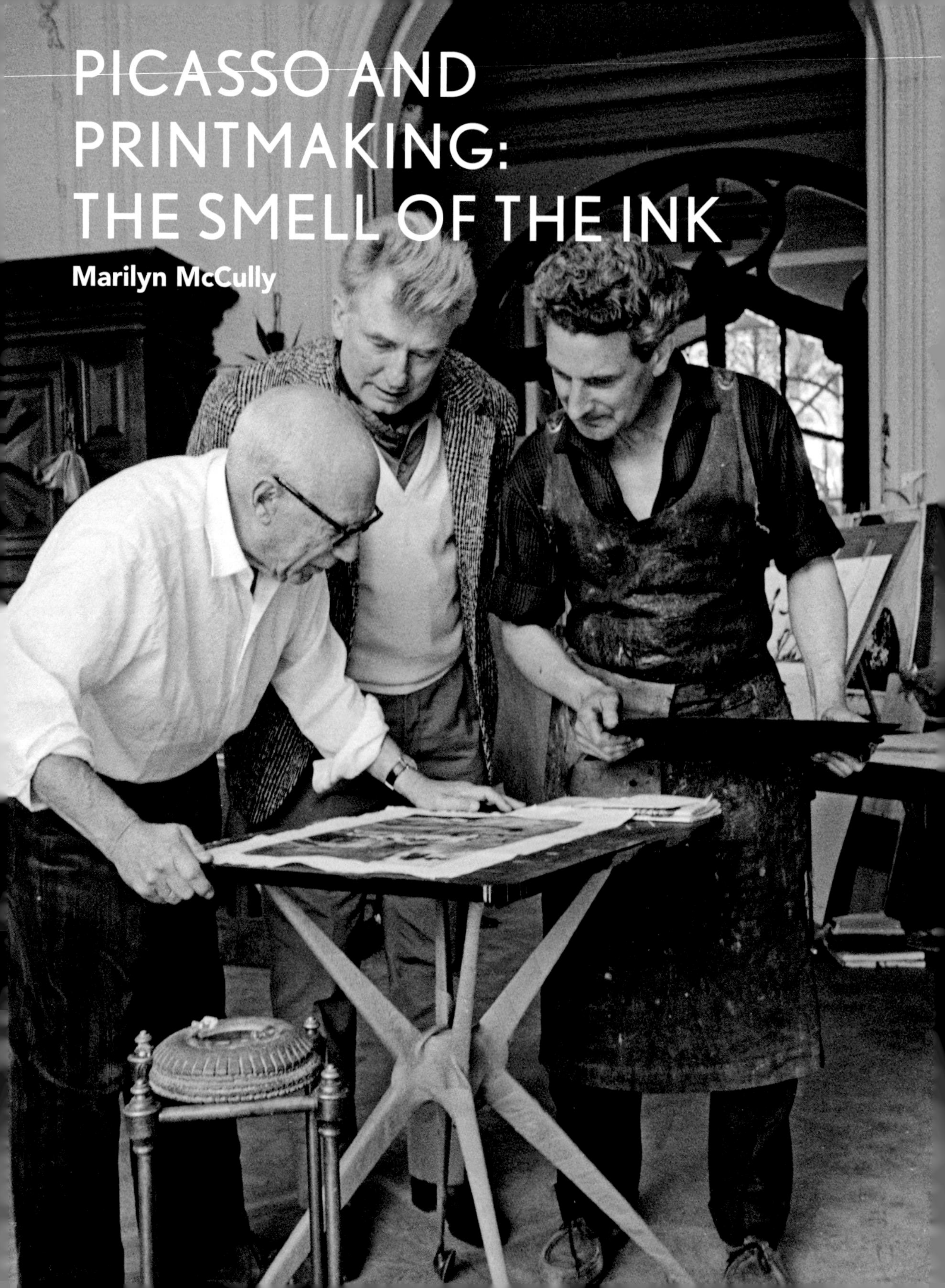

PICASSO AND PRINTMAKING: THE SMELL OF THE INK

Marilyn McCully

The reputation of Pablo Picasso (1881–1973) as one of the twentieth century's most creative and forward-looking painters is
unrivaled. At the same time, the less familiar fact of the pleasure
he took in his collaborations with artisans and technicians
broadens our understanding of his overall artistic practice and
achievements. Indeed, this modern master seems to have had
a certain nostalgic identification with working people (a pose
he had adopted in his dress as a young man in Paris), especially
when it came to entering into the production line of a pottery
factory, a sculptor's atelier, or a print shop. But once he achieved
the technical skills that he required, his competitive desire to
take things one stage further always led him to push the bound-
aries of the different media that he explored. Moreover, his
approach—no matter how unconventional—was always directed
at the artistic effects that he could achieve and, unlike some of
his contemporaries, such as the Dadaist Francis Picabia (1879–
1953), not planned as a provocation. Even at the height of the
development of Cubism, for instance, when Picasso incorporat-
ed housepaint into his paintings—something that offended
traditionally trained artists, including his close colleague Georges
Braque (1882–1963)—his aim was to render the textures of
specific objects, including flags and labels, as closely as possible
to the real thing without resorting to the imitative use of traditional materials. In the field of printmaking, Picasso learned
from the experts and then always took every process to its limit
and beyond.

Picasso's first major print was *The Frugal Repast* (cat. no. 2),
an etching that was carried out in his Bateau Lavoir studio in
Montmartre during the late summer of 1904. The subject—two
figures seated at a table, with a piece of bread, an empty bowl,
and a bottle in front of them—is still imbued with the sense
of poverty and isolation that had characterized his Blue Period
compositions of the previous year.[1]

When the artist's model Fernande Olivier (1881–1966) first
visited Picasso's studio that summer, she remembered seeing
The Frugal Repast in progress: "He's working on an etching
showing an emaciated man and woman seated at a table in a
wine shop, who convey an intense feeling of misery and alcohol-
ism with terrifying realism."[2] The man, who looks away from his
companion, wears a predominantly dark top, while the woman

wears a lighter outfit, and this light-dark contrast heightens the sense of their psychological separation in the bleak interior setting.

The zinc plate that served as the basis for *The Frugal Repast* had been given to Picasso by the artist Joan González (1868–1908) sometime after his arrival in Paris in April 1904, probably when Picasso is thought to have stayed with Joan and his brother Julio González (1876–1942) in Montparnasse for several days before taking over the studio in the Bateau Lavoir.[3] Joan had previously worked on the large plate, and although the surface was scraped down before Picasso started, traces of a landscape by another hand are still visible at the upper right. Nonetheless, the results of Picasso's exploration of the techniques of etching in *The Frugal Repast* are remarkable.[4] The deep blacks that he obtained allowed him to articulate the features and hands of the two figures with sharp shadows and a sense of modeling, while highlights on both the man and the woman were done with a scraper (*grattoir*). Touches of black on the white tablecloth not only convey the effect of wrinkles but also establish a rhythm to the tabletop that contrasts with the solidity of the objects placed on its surface.

For printing, Picasso went to Eugène Delâtre (1864–1938), whose studio on rue Lepic, just around the corner from the Bateau Lavoir, was well known among artists in Montmartre. Delâtre had famously been the printer for Henri de Toulouse-Lautrec (1864–1901), Auguste Renoir (1841–1919), and others, and had himself achieved a considerable reputation as an artist-printmaker in the late nineteenth century.[5] Delâtre pulled a first proof of *The Frugal Repast* in which the background is fairly unified and light, and the face and right shoulder of the man are relatively bright.[6] Picasso then reworked certain areas of the plate, including the face of the man and his bony shoulders, and he settled on the second state, in which the background is dramatically articulated with a curving shadow at the left.

At a time when Picasso was usually short of funds, printmaking offered him an opportunity to make some money by selling multiple works at reasonably low prices and, at the same time, to circulate his name among artistic circles in both Barcelona and Paris. Of the first group of trial proofs of *The Frugal Repast*, he made a gift of one to his Barcelona friend Sebastià Junyent (1865–1908) in the hope that Junyent would be able to sell others

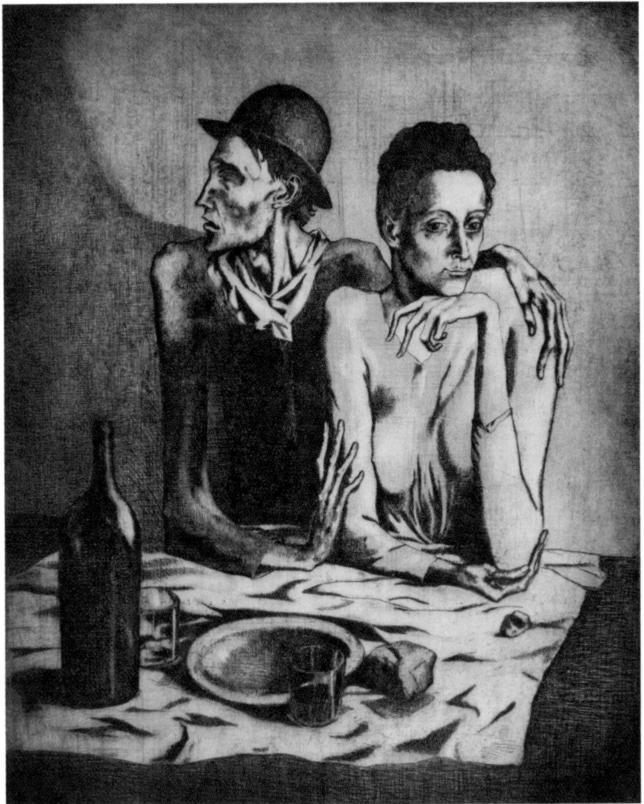

Fig. 17

on his behalf. [7] Three of the first impressions, one of which is now in the Art Institute of Chicago (fig. 17), were also proofed in Prussian blue. In some respects, *The Frugal Repast* stands as a farewell to the Blue Period. Picasso's subsequent work, including oils, gouaches, drawings, and prints, reflected not only a shift in subject matter but also a brighter tonality. He continued making drypoints and etchings over the winter of 1904–5, again in the hope that works on paper might attract buyers, and these prints included a couple of portraits as well as compositions in which the subject of the circus and traveling performers predominated.

In his exhibition at the Galeries Serrurier, which was held in late February 1905, Picasso included several prints, listed in the catalogue as two *étampes* (presumably drypoints) and an unspecified number of *eau-fortes* (etchings). In a little sketchbook that contains references to the paintings and frames for the Serrurier show,[8] Picasso made a note to himself (fig. 18): *tirar pruevas puntas secas* (pull drypoint proofs). This would likely have been done at Delâtre's atelier, probably shortly before the final Serrurier selection was made. Pierre Daix has suggested that *The Frugal Repast* was in the exhibition, but the other prints cannot all be identified,[9] though in a later review of the show, Guillaume Apollinaire (1880–1918) spoke of the poetic means that Picasso employed, notably in drypoints, to convey the struggles of itinerant performers to make ends meet.[10]

Related to this group of prints of traveling acrobats (known as *saltimbanques*) is another of the drypoints that Delâtre pulled for Picasso in 1905, the evocative composition known as *Salomé* (cat. no. 3), which he worked on in the summer. The huge, seated Herod, who is positioned at the upper left and for whom Salomé is dancing—a servant holds the head of John the Baptist at the lower right—can be related to drawings of a *saltimbanque* or clown in a sketchbook Picasso had with him in Holland (late June–early July 1905). This figure relates to the strongman in Picasso's major painting of that year, *Family of Saltimbanques* (see fig. 22), which was completed in the summer. Picasso continued working with Delâtre until the mid-1920s, but he later claimed that he was always frustrated by the printer's practice of prohibiting him from entering the atelier when prints were being pulled.[11] Beginning in 1913, the artist began a collaboration with Louis Fort (1866–1950), who had been commissioned by the dealer Ambroise Vollard (1866–1939) to steel-face Picasso's early plates, which Vollard had acquired two years earlier. Fort produced new impressions of these prints, including *The Frugal Repast* and *Salomé*.

Around 1907, Picasso is thought to have acquired a hand press, which he kept in his Bateau Lavoir studio. As Brigitte Baer has pointed out, between that date and 1932 he experimented with printing techniques primarily on his own, and he went to Louis Fort when it came to biting the plates.[12] During the early and mid-1920s he also proofed a number of etchings and engravings himself on Louis Fort's press, but the majority of these were not issued as editions at the time. The striking *Portrait of Olga in a Fur Collar* (cat. no. 6), which represents the artist's first wife, the Russian dancer Olga Khokhlova (1891–1955), for instance, was originally carried out in 1923 but only printed by Fort in 1930.[13] Not only is the size of the print impressive (the zinc plate measures

Fig. 18

　　　　McCully

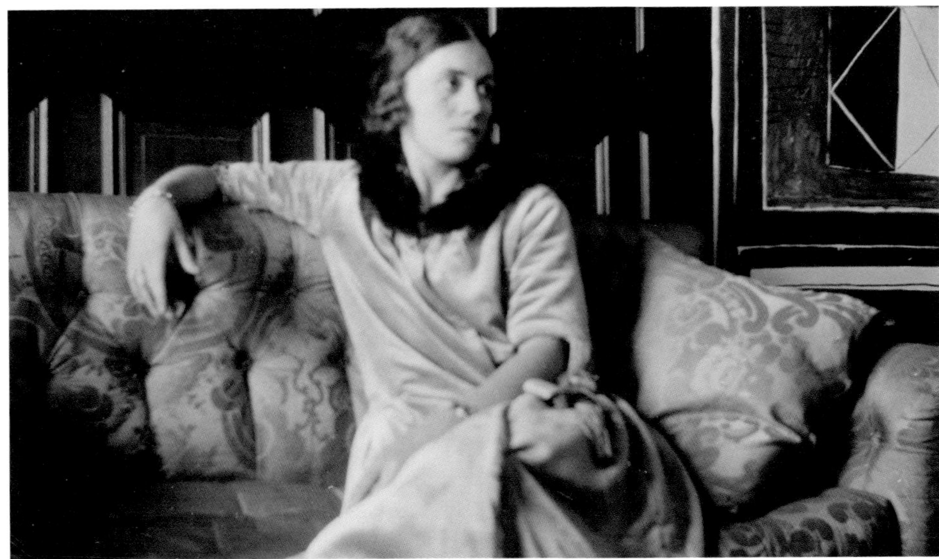

Fig. 19

19 ½ × 19 ⅜ inches), but there is also a sense of monumentality in the composition itself, with the head and shoulders of Olga filling the central space. The artist's mastery of drypoint line, principally through cross-hatching, conveys a strong sense of modeling in the face and neck, while delicate marks suggest the soft fur collar juxtaposed against the contour lines of her face at the left. Photographs (fig. 19) and paintings of this period often show Olga wearing the same fur-trimmed dress.[14]

Several of Picasso's subsequent undertakings with Fort included the printing of the illustrations for two important books: *Le Chef-d'oeuvre inconnu d'Honoré de Balzac* (1927) and Ovid's *Les Métamorphoses* (1931). When Fort retired at the end of 1932, Picasso bought his press and had it installed at Boisgeloup, the château northwest of Paris that he had acquired in 1930, and when he moved to a new studio on rue des Grands Augustins in Paris in 1937, he took the press with him.[15]

The decade of the 1930s represents a period of concentrated activity in printmaking for Picasso, and his collaboration with Roger Lacourière (1892–1966) marks an essential step forward in his mastery of and experimentation with different printing methods. The Atelier Lacourière had been established in 1929 on rue

Fig. 18
Pablo Picasso, Page from *Carnet 35*, 1905. Crayon, 5 ¾ × 3 ½ in. (14.5 × 9 cm). Private Collection

Fig. 19
Photograph of Olga in the living room at 23, rue la Boétie, c. 1922.

Foyatier in Montmartre, and Picasso began working there regularly after Fort's retirement. He especially enjoyed his collaboration with Lacourière, who was instrumental in introducing him to various techniques, including classic and sugar-lift aquatint. The Atelier Lacourière also took over some of the time-consuming workshop tasks, such as preparing plates and pulling proofs, with the result that Picasso's own work went that much faster, and he forged ahead "mistreating" or "misusing" conventional techniques in order to arrive at the results he desired. Baer observed that "his burin, his etching needle, and his scraper are used with so much force that it seems as if he wanted to gouge right through the copper."[16]

Work on Picasso's most celebrated engraving, the *Minotauromachia* (cat. no. 11), was carried out at the Atelier Lacourière, beginning on March 23, 1935. The composition went through seven states, with significant changes made to some of the figures and to the intensity and contrast of dark and light in the overall scene.[17] The complex subject matter anticipates the violence of *Guernica* (1937; fig. 20), and the use of etching and engraving techniques is equally dramatic. The Minotaur, with its enormous bull's head and muscular man's body (with a tail), enters from the right, while at the left a slender, Christ-like figure climbs a ladder. Next to him a little girl holds a bouquet of flowers and gestures with a lit candle in her other hand toward the Minotaur. Filling the space between these characters is an image taken from the bullfight— the crumpled body of a wounded or dead *rejoneadora* (female bullfighter) with her horse beneath her. By leaving parts of the surface untouched, Picasso illuminates certain areas of the composition, emphasizing the innocence and courage that the child represents and the stillness of the *rejoneadora* (whose profile resembles the artist's mistress Marie-Thérèse Walter [1909–1977]) in the center. In contrast to these areas, the rest of the plate is etched with myriad lines defining the patterns of the *rejoneadora's* suit of lights,[18] the curls of the Minotaur's hairy head, the precisely rendered matador's sword, rain beginning to fall from the sky, and many other details, all of which heighten the haunting qualities and mystery of the powerful scene.

The setting of the *Minotauromachia*, however, is not a bullfight arena but a beach on the seashore (a tiny boat appears on the horizon), which, in Picasso's work, is the place where mythological

Fig. 20
Pablo Picasso, *Guernica*, 1937. Oil on canvas, 137 ½ × 305 ¾ in. (349.3 × 776.6 cm). Museo nacional centro de arte Reina Sofía, Madrid, DE00050

McCully

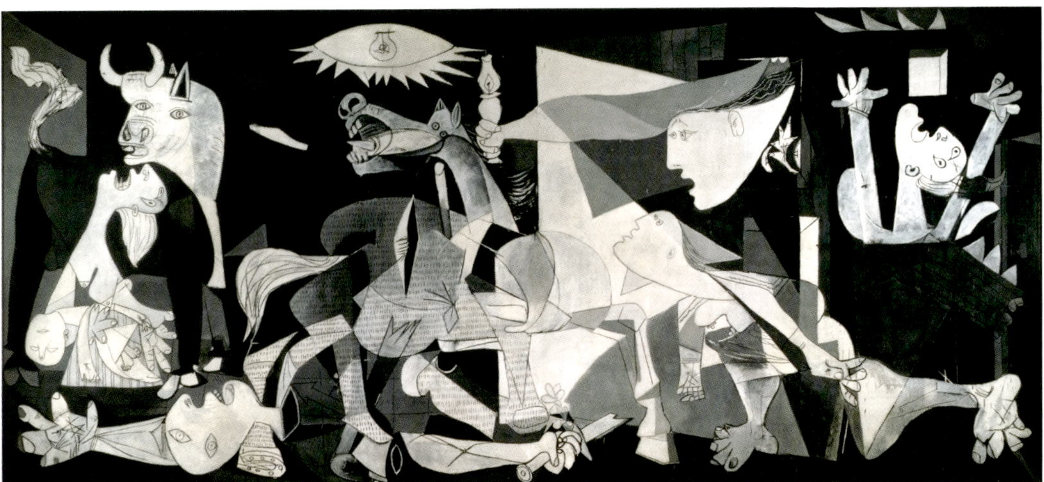

Fig. 20

creatures often appear. At the upper left, two female spectators and a dove can be seen looking out from an arched window of an otherwise undefined building. In *Guernica* these women are transformed into victims trapped by the fires of bombed buildings in the Basque town, and a horse and fallen warrior, rather than the *rejoneadora*, occupy the lower part of the composition. The similarity of the two images is even more striking when one takes into account that the scene as Picasso worked on it is reversed in the final print.

In the early 1940s, Picasso continued collaborating with Lacourière, sometimes providing him with work to keep his atelier from closing completely during wartime. Jacques Frélaut (1913–1997) became head of the atelier soon afterward and continued the association with Picasso well into the early 1960s.[19] Frélaut also installed Louis Fort's press in the basement of Picasso's villa La Californie in Cannes in 1957, and he recalled the artist's delight at having re-created a version of the Atelier Lacourière on his own premises. Frélaut described the challenge that working with copper plates and printmaking tools still represented for Picasso at that time: "He needed to have command of his medium, to tame it. He was a brawler, he was always competitive. 'If I'd been a shoemaker,' he once said to me, 'I'd have wanted to be the one who made the largest number of shoes!'"[20] When Picasso moved out of La Californie in 1961, Frélaut was called upon again to help with packing up all of the artist's printmaking paraphernalia, which included a box with engraved copper and zinc plates dating back to the 1920s. Picasso later asked Frélaut to proof them so that he could choose which ones he would like to have printed as editions, but Frélaut actually went ahead and produced editions from all of the plates. A few of these were issued, but most of them were hidden away in a box that the artist referred to as his *caisse à remords* (conscience box) and were only numbered and sold after his death.

In addition to his activity in engraving in the 1940s, Picasso began directing his attention to the medium of lithography, and his collaboration with Fernand Mourlot (1895–1988) in this undertaking would prove extremely fruitful. Along with two of his brothers, Mourlot had taken over the printing press of their father in 1921, naming their Paris atelier Mourlot Frères, which was originally located on rue Chabrol, near the Gare du Nord. He remembered his first meeting with Picasso in October 1945: "He loved the printing works, the noise of the machines, the smell of the ink, the contact with the workers."[21] He also recalled that Picasso loved probing the limits of the lithographic medium, even if his efforts went against standard methods. In the beginning he worked on transfer paper and also directly on stone with wax crayons, wash drawing, and other techniques, but the technicians were reportedly astounded by his neglect of traditional practices. Picasso would often rework the stone after the first proofs had been pulled, scraping and marking the surface with lithographic crayon and ink. "After this sort of treatment the design generally becomes indecipherable and is destroyed. But, with him! Each time it would turn out very well. Why? That's a mystery…"[22]

Mourlot recalled that one of his most memorable early collaborations with Picasso was the printing of *David and Bathsheba, after Cranach* (cat. no. 19), which was begun on March 30, 1947, and was originally carried out with brushes and ink on a zinc plate. The composition was based on a black-and-white reproduction in a catalogue that Picasso's dealer Daniel-Henry Kahnweiler (1884–1979) had given him of a Lucas Cranach (1472–1553) exhibition in Berlin.[23] In his interpretation of Cranach's scene, Picasso focused as much of his attention on the bearded David and his male attendants, who watch from a rooftop above, as he did on the group of female figures surrounding Bathsheba bathing below. Indeed, he departs from the biblical story (2 Samuel 11) in that

David's voyeuristic gaze seems to be fixed on the standing attendant behind Bathsheba rather than on the seated figure herself. This tall woman bears a resemblance to the artist's companion Françoise Gilot (b. 1921),[24] and her attire, especially in the later states of the lithograph, evokes the series of lithographic portraits that Picasso did of Gilot wearing an embroidered jacket at the turn of 1948–49.

Shortly after beginning *David and Bathsheba, after Cranach*, however, Picasso abandoned the zinc plate and put it aside, only taking it up again a year later. Once he resumed work, there would be further states, in which he inked over the original image and redrew the design. After the sixth state, he asked Mourlot to bring a lithographic stone to his studio so that the composition could be transferred from zinc to stone. With some trepidation, according to Mourlot, Picasso then attacked the stone, using a number of different lithographic techniques, including much scraping, and he paid special attention to reworking the blacks.[25] Before leaving Paris for the summer in June 1949, he asked Mourlot to print a proof of what would turn out to be the definitive state (cat. no. 20). The different processes Picasso employed, including the removal of earlier inking, accounts for the great changes between the different states.[26]

Picasso's well-known *Dove* (cat. no. 21), which is dated January 9, 1949, was done with lithographic ink on zinc, and the flowing application of the wash enhances the naturalistic qualities of the bird with its soft white feathers. Picasso's dove (as well as other variations of the bird) was adopted at this time as emblematic of the Peace Movement. In fact, Mourlot printed this particular *Dove* on the poster for the Congrès Mondial des Partisans de la Paix (World Peace Conference), which was held at the Salle Pleyel in Paris in April 1949 (fig. 21). However, pigeons or doves also had personal significance for the artist: when he was a child, his father had kept pigeons, and Picasso himself would do the same when he later moved to La Californie in Cannes. Moreover, in Picasso's ceramics of this same period, he frequently populated the surfaces of plates with painted or carved images of doves, and he transformed clay bottles into imaginative sculptural renderings of the bird. In this connection, it is important to note that Picasso took enormous pleasure in his interaction with the skilled workers at the Madoura pottery in Vallauris, where he had

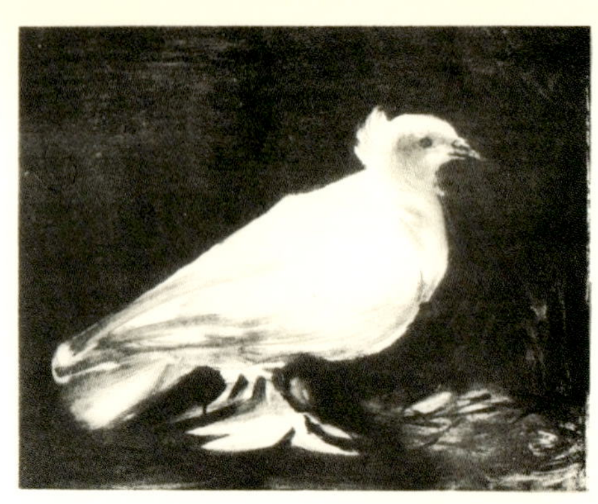

Fig. 21

begun producing ceramics regularly in 1947, just as he had with the machine minders at Mourlot's atelier in Paris. The delight he took in breaking the rules of ceramic decoration and reinventing age-old techniques would produce unrivaled results over the course of many years.

When he was in Vallauris, Picasso's preference for zinc plates rather than stone for his lithographs was due primarily to physical circumstances. Stones would have been too cumbersome and heavy to transport, so Mourlot would bring the plates from Paris. Lacking any other appropriate space, Picasso would usually work on them on the floor of the Madoura pottery. Mourlot would then pack up the plates and take them back to Paris for proofing. The portrait of Picasso's daughter Paloma (b. 1949) with her doll (cat. no. 24), for example, is one of three lithographic variations

McCully

on the same subject that were executed in Vallauris in December 1952, when the artist's daughter was only three. Mourlot recalled that these compositions were done on zinc, using lithographic crayon and Seccotine (a brand of household glue), convenient materials the artist had at hand, to produce the resists—according to Mourlot, "an original process to say the least."[27]

After Picasso acquired the villa La Galloise in Vallauris (1949), apart from a few months each year when he returned to Paris, he concentrated his artistic activity in the south of France. The villa was within walking distance of the Madoura pottery, and nearby he also acquired an old perfume factory, Le Fournas, where he experimented with assemblage sculptures. Living in the town brought him into contact with other local artists, among them a German, Franz Schneider (1901–1971), whom Picasso had originally met at the Paris Peace Conference in 1949. Schneider had gone to Vallauris in 1953,[28] and he and Picasso, along with the photographer André Villers (French, 1930–2016), formed a little *tertulia*,[29] getting together to talk about art, bullfights, and life in the small town.[30] On one occasion, Picasso discussed his impatience at the time delay between working on lithographs in Vallauris and their proofing in Paris. Schneider encouraged him to try linocut, a technique he himself had learned in Germany.[31] This suggestion would lead to Picasso's subsequent collaboration with the local Vallauris printer Hidalgo Arnéra (1922–2007), with whom he began by producing posters for ceramics exhibitions and bullfights, starting in 1954. Their work together over the course of the next few years would result in an inventive use of the linocut process that enabled Picasso to extend the parameters of yet another printmaking technique.

Arnéra had originally trained in his father's print shop in Vallauris, and during the war he had learned linocut techniques in Austria as part of his *travail obligatoire*.[32] When he returned to the south of France, he worked for a while in a small print shop in Cannes, where he specialized in typography, but he later took over his father's shop in Vallauris. After Picasso moved to Cannes in 1955 with his future wife Jacqueline Roque Hutin (1927–1986), he and Arnéra began their close collaboration on the linocut process: Picasso would work on the lino blocks at La Californie, and the different states would be taken to Vallauris for color proofing. Arnéra told an interviewer: "Picasso worked at night; in the morning,

Marcel the chauffeur brought what he had completed to the print shop with notes added by Jacqueline Roque. I pulled the proofs and returned them to La Californie at exactly 1:30. This regular rhythm of working continued for eight years, every day, except Saturday and Sunday. If Picasso gave his approval, the proof was printed the next day. The next color could be printed two or three days later. In the meantime Picasso worked on other subjects."[33]

The opportunity to experiment with the medium of linocut especially appealed to Picasso, who wanted to produce prints that would allow him to work freely with color. One of the most spectacular early linocuts that he produced with Arnéra is *Portrait of a Young Girl, after Cranach the Younger, II* (cat. no. 28). Baer has noted that for reference to the original painting, Picasso worked from a postcard reproduction.[34] In the case of Picasso's interpretation, five linoleum blocks were used for the different colors (bistre, yellow, red, blue, and black), which were superimposed one after another for the printing. The black plate, although printed last, was cut first, as the master on which the other plates were based. A level of transparency in the inks allowed new tints to be formed by superimposition: the sleeves, for example, are solid in the blue plate, and the blue pattern appears where the bistre plate has been cut away, with the color of the surrounding fabric created by blue over bistre. The intensity of the blacks comes from the solidity of these areas in all the plates (except yellow), while the yellow is allowed to shine through voids in the other plates in the gold necklace and decoration of the hair.

However, Picasso found the process of using so many different plates cumbersome, and in collaboration with Arnéra, he adopted a process whereby the different plates were created by successively cutting more and more away from just one or two blocks of linoleum. For *Still Life with Hanging Lamp* (cat. no. 31), one plate, cut only to leave the whites of the light bulb, the nail, and the glass, was used to print a unified gray image over a creamy white ground. This was overprinted six times with the ever-diminishing surface of the second plate, in matte black, yellow, green, red, pale blue, and—to strengthen some of the outlines of the foreground still life—with shiny black ink. This means that there is yellow beneath all the green, red, and blue areas; green beneath the red and blue; etc. This was a technique that had been used before by poster artists, but the sophistication of Picasso's design demanded an extraordinary feat of visualization of the final image, since each stage was definitive and could not be changed or reworked later.

Picasso's last significant printmaking collaboration was with the Crommelynck brothers, Aldo (1931–2008) and Piero (1934–2001), who in 1963 set up a printing works in the old bakery in Mougins, near Picasso's last studio at Notre-Dame-de-Vie. Over the course of the next nine years, they would work with him on some 750 prints, and the artist's innovative and constantly probing combination of techniques provided them as printers with a constant challenge. Piero Crommelynck understood that for Picasso printmaking "represented not only the amazing effort of the craftsman but also something less definable, more profound."[35]

The Crommelyncks were sons of the Belgian playwright Fernand Crommelynck,[36] who had sent them with their brother Milan in the early 1950s to work in the Atelier Lacourière. There they not only learned their trade as printers, but also came into contact with Picasso himself. The possibilities of direct collaboration with him led Aldo and Piero to move to the south of France. This suited Picasso quite well, since, apart from his activity with Arnéra on linocuts, he had been compelled to send his engraved or lithographic plates for other prints back to Paris for proofing. Now this aspect of the process could be done on site, reducing the time between the proofing and his continuing to work on a particular composition, which he was always anxious to do. Geographic proximity also allowed him to be in direct contact with the Crommelyncks, so that he was free to discuss both technical matters as he worked and also the next stages that he wished to carry out. "He worked with extraordinary freedom, accomplishing amazing technical feats, and seemed to be unfettered by any rules that might restrict his spontaneity, even though printmaking was always said to be stubbornly resistant to improvisation."[37]

The so-called *Suite 347* (1968) was done over a period of seven months and represents the largest and, in many ways, most impressive suite of engravings that the artist ever produced. In addition to the different levels of technical experimentation that the artist carried out with the Crommelyncks, the complexity of the scenes within the suite is astounding, including many direct references to Picasso's own life and art, as well as to art history and literature. Picasso remarked about the genesis of imagery in the *Suite 347*: "Of course, one never knows what's going to come out, but as soon as the drawing gets under way, a story or an idea is born, and that's it. Then the story grows, like theater or life— and the drawing is turned into other drawings, a real novel."[38]

The first plate (cat. no. 37) in the suite features a circus setting that reverberates with echoes of the artist's 1905 fascination and identification with the lives of traveling performers. Not only had he depicted *saltimbanques* in his prints, he memorably included a self-portrait, as an acrobat dressed in Harlequin's costume, among the troupe that he portrayed in the large oil painting *Family of Saltimbanques* (fig. 22). Over sixty years later, he would again insert himself into this world of popular entertainment, this time as an old clown at the left, in the company of his wife Jacqueline. Across the foreground, they face a bearded acrobat— an allusion to Picasso's youth and his early identification with *saltimbanques*—at the right.

In the center of the circus ring is a horseback rider, whose appearance in the composition makes reference to Picasso's memory of his first Barcelona girlfriend, the *equestrienne* Rosita del Oro. At the same time, her acrobatic display on horseback also evokes the appearance of female bullfighters, who are frequently represented in the artist's work of the 1930s (cat. no. 9). Around the central characters, Picasso fills practically all available space with members of the audience, and in the final state their heads are reduced to minimal lines, with dark spots for their eyes and mouths. Another significant change that occurs in the different states is the appearance of a small rearing horse at the lower right. This animal is absent from the first state, but over the next three stages, it is developed as a counterpoint to the reclining youth in the foreground. However, as he worked on the plate, Picasso changed his mind about including this horse at all and returned to his initial idea. He scratched out much of the area at the right and superimposed heavy blacks, and only traces of the creature's legs are visible in the final composition.

As Picasso developed the *Suite 347*, creating an imaginative narrative from one scene to the next, he also worked with a variety of techniques, including experiments in aquatint and scraping, sometimes combining them with burin and other engraving methods in unorthodox and unexpected ways.

McCully

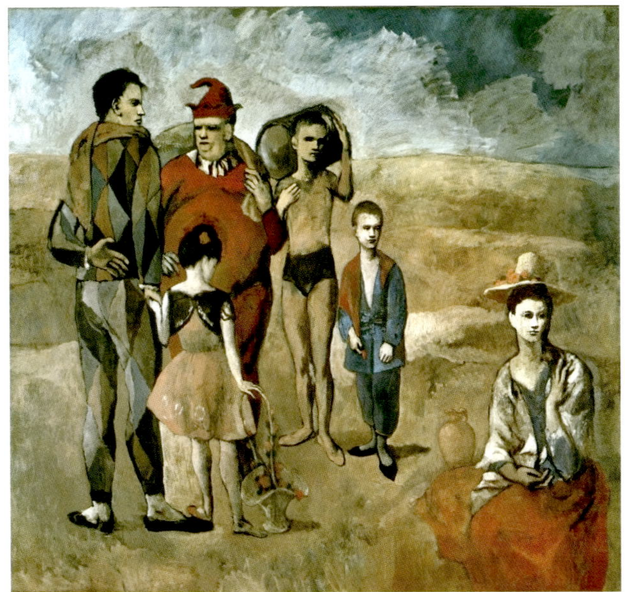

Fig. 22

The close and friendly relationship with the Crommelyncks
continued, and in 1970 Picasso would produce yet another
important suite, known as *156 Engravings*. This series was begun
in early January 1970, and includes yet more references to
Picasso's life as an artist, to his favorite artists in the past, and to
literature. On February 19, for instance, he recreated a scene
from Guy de Maupassant's (1850–1893) *Maison Tellier*,[39] which
had been interpreted before him by Edgar Degas (1834–1917)
in a series of monotypes that Picasso actually owned. In this case,
according to Piero Crommelynck, the artist wanted to create an
engraving that bypassed the need for a proof stage, much in
the same way that a monotype would have been executed in one
effort: "He wanted to avoid the peril that is often encountered
when an etching goes through a succession of states, when the
initial line is almost submerged when it is covered with the varnish,
and the point of the needle is diverted by the previous bite of
the acid."[40]

Nevertheless, in the case of the *156 Engravings* series, Picasso
worked with the Crommelyncks to proof different states of
specific images, especially when it came to complex and chang-
ing compositions. An extraordinary example is the engraving

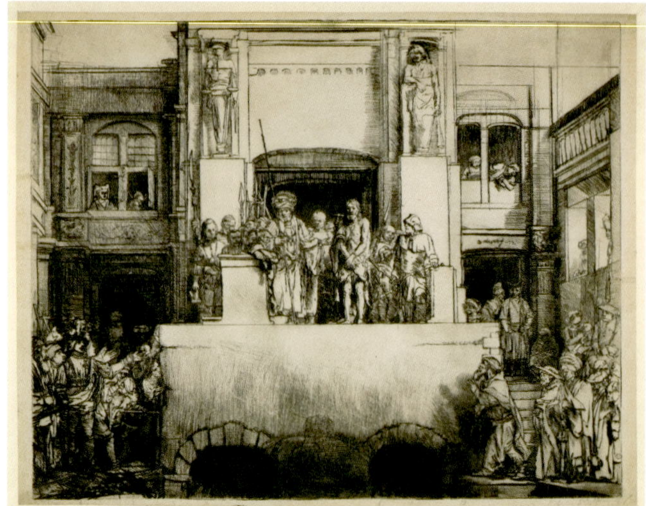

Fig. 23

Fig. 23
Rembrandt van Rijn (Dutch, 1606–
1669), *Christ Presented to the People
(Ecce Homo)*, 1655. Drypoint on
paper, 15 ¼ × 17 ⅞ in. (38.8 ×
45.5 cm). Scottish National Gallery,
Edinburgh, P 114

known as *Ecce Homo, after Rembrandt* (no. 10 in the series; cat.
no. 38). The scene is based on a Rembrandt van Rijn (1606–1669)
drypoint showing Christ presented to the people (fig. 23). The
combination of architectural elements, strong contrasts of light
and dark, and the centrality of the group featuring Pilate and
Christ on a stage in the Rembrandt drypoint are compositionally
compelling and add drama to the religious scene. In Rembrandt's
case, the artist simplified the composition through the different
states—that is, removing rather than adding figures in the foreground and replacing them with two dungeon-like arches in the
wall.[41] What Picasso does is successively transform the stage
into a theater, like the earliest states of Rembrandt's print, with
the king (Pilate) seated on a throne in the center, surrounded by
his attendants, including nudes (both female and male) and,
once again, a woman on horseback. In front and at the sides of
this strongly lit stage are the people, who seem to fill every bit
of the space (apart from the upper right, where Picasso dated the
work and noted that it was the seventh state). The relative sizes
and scale of the different types who make up the audience are
inconsistent, and among the nudes, youths, and bearded figures
are a number of women, some of whom, especially in the foreground, resemble Picasso's wife, Jacqueline. Another female
head in profile, with her head thrown back, stands out among the
others in the foreground, and her anguished expression strangely

McCully

merges with the face with closed eyes above her. In this way, the emotional component in Picasso's composition derives from the force of artistic invention and juxtaposition. Work on the series continued into 1971, and the last print to be included in the series of *156 Engravings* was actually completed on March 25, 1972, just a little over a year before the artist died at the age of ninety-one.

Picasso had learned traditional methods of painting and drawing as a student in Spain, but over the course of his long career, he always relished the opportunity to collaborate with printers, artisans, and metalworkers in order to expand his technical understanding of working in other media. As Mourlot recounted, he loved the atmosphere of the atelier, and he profited from working alongside the skilled technicians. His willingness to enter into this aspect of the printing process differs markedly from many artists, including his old friend and rival, Henri Matisse (1869–1954). Mourlot remembered that Matisse only came once to the lithography atelier, and, in general, he preferred to leave matters of printing complete-ly in the hands of the technicians, and he was always addressed respectfully as "*maître.*"[42] Picasso, on the other hand, regarded his work with printers as part of the realization of his art.

Printmaking in Picasso's early career had represented a means of earning money and establishing his reputation, but it also offered him the opportunity to extend the range of his formal investiga-tions in a variety of media. Later in life, printmaking assumed an even more meaningful role on a personal level, allowing him not only to create narratives but also to ponder the whole of his creative career in the context of the history of art, including references to artists and printmakers, such as Rembrandt, who had inspired him. Making art was fundamental to Picasso at every moment in his life, and he prided himself on the broad range of skills and techniques that he had mastered, often through associations with his collabora-tors, over so many years. When Picasso was eighty-nine, he asked the photographer Edward Quinn (1920–1997) to film him making a drypoint in order to demonstrate the steadiness of his hand.[43] The challenge and pursuit of art kept him alive to the very end.

NOTES

Unless indicated otherwise, English translations of quoted passages are by the author.

1. Between 1902 and 1904, blue was the predominant color in Picasso's oil paintings, whose subject matter referred to the isolated lives of marginal people.

2. Fernande Olivier, *Loving Picasso* (New York: Abrams, 2001), 139.

3. Picasso first knew the González brothers in Barcelona, before they settled in Paris. A letter of June 14, 1904, to Picasso from a mutual Barcelona friend (Sebastià Junyer Vidal) was sent to him at the González brothers' Montparnasse address (Archives Picasso, Musée national Picasso-Paris).

4. Although he had never formally studied printmaking, he learned a certain amount in Barcelona from the artist Ricard Canals, under whose instruction he is thought to have executed his first etching, *El Zurdo*, 1899 (Baer 1).

5. Brigitte Baer, whose catalogue raisonné is an indispensable source of information for Picasso's activity as a printmaker, believes that Eugène Delâtre's father, Auguste, himself a master printer, may well have given Picasso advice at the time he was working on *The Frugal Repast*; see her excellent essay, "The Hand, the Manner," in Brigitte Baer, *Picasso the Engraver: Selections from the Musée Picasso, Paris*, exh. cat. (New York: Metropolitan Museum of Art, September 18–December 21, 1997), 55–75.

6. Baer 2.1; Musée national Picasso-Paris.

7. The example he gave to Sebastià Junyent is inscribed "September 1904," providing a date for the completion of the print; see John Richardson, *A Life of Picasso*, vol. 1 (New York: Random House, 1991), 301.

8. The sketchbook, known as Carnet 35, has been broken up since it was first exhibited as part of Marina Picasso's collection; see E. A. Carmean, "The Saltimbanques: Sketchbook No. 35, 1905," in *Je suis le cahier: The Sketchbooks of Picasso*, ed. Arnold Glimcher and Marc Glimcher, exh. cat. (New York: Pace Gallery, May 2–August 1, 1986), 9–50.

9. Pierre Daix and Georges Boudaille, *Picasso: The Blue and Rose Periods* (Greenwich, CT: New York Graphic Society, 1967), 255.

10. Apollinaire's review appeared in *La Plume*, May 15, 1905.

11. Baer, "The Hand, the Manner," 60.

12. Baer, "The Hand, the Manner," 55.

13. In 1955, further proofs were pulled by Roger Lacourière.

14. See, for example, the oil on canvas *Portrait de femme au col de fourrure (Olga)*, 1922–23, on loan to the Museo Picasso Málaga.

15. Louis Fort retired to Golfe-Juan, near Antibes. When Picasso and Françoise Gilot were together in the south of France in 1946, they stayed in Fort's house.

16. Baer, "The Hand, the Manner," 56.

17. Details of the different states and proofs are given in Brigitte Baer, *Picasso, Peintre-Graveur*, vol. 3 (Bern: Kornfeld, 1986), entry for no. 573. Additional information is given in Brigitte Baer, *Picasso, Peintre-Graveur: Addendum aux tomes I à VII* (Bern: Kornfeld, 1996), 28–32.

18. The traditional bullfighter's costume is called a *traje de luces* (suit of lights). During the bullfight its elaborate metallic decoration reflects the sun.

19. From 1957 the printing works became known as the Atelier Lacourière-Frélaut.

20. Quoted in French and Spanish in *La línea ininterrumpida. Picasso, Fin, Vilató, Xavier*, exh. cat. (Málaga: Museo Casa Natal, Málaga, October 22, 2015–January 24, 2016), 29. My thanks to Marta-Volga de Minteguiaga-Guezala, curator of the Málaga exhibition, for sharing her knowledge of the Atelier Lacourière-Frélaut with me.

21. Fernand Mourlot, *Gravés dans ma mémoire* (Paris: Robert Laffont, 1979), 24.

22. According to Jean Célestin, who worked with Picasso at the Mourlot atelier; quoted in Hélène Parmelin's introduction to Fernand Mourlot, *Picasso Lithographs*, trans. Jean Didry (Paris: Boston Book and Art Publisher, 1970), [3].

23. Susan Galassi, *Picasso's Variations on the Masters* (New York: Abrams, 1996), 100 and 213, n. 55.

24. Galassi identifies David in the composition as a surrogate for Picasso and Bathsheba as Françoise (*Picasso's Variations*, 110).

25. Mourlot, *Gravés dans ma mémoire*, 30.

26. For a full account of the work on both zinc and stone, see Felix Reuße, *Pablo Picasso: Die Lithographie* (Münster: Graphikmuseum Pablo Picasso, 2000), 82–88.

27. Mourlot, *Gravés dans ma mémoire*, 196.

28. Franz Schneider was born Carl Franz Schneider in Saarbrücken, where he trained in decorative arts. He later referred to himself either as François Schneider (in France) or simply as Schnei. In a letter of April 23, 1953, he informed "comrade Picasso" that he was in Vallauris and that he hoped to see him again (Archives Picasso, Musée national Picasso-Paris). Afterward, at Picasso's suggestion, Schneider took up ceramics, working in the Vallauris studio of the potter Blaise Rubino.

29. A *tertulia* is the regular get-together in Spain of a group of like-minded friends and colleagues, to discuss life, work, politics, and local or cultural affairs.

30. Villers photographed the group at the bar known as les Charlet in Vallauris in 1953. In addition to the Charlet couple at the back, seated at the table at Picasso's right is the bullfighter Minuni, and on his left is Schneider; see *Picasso dans l'œil de Villers*, exh. cat. (Paris: Galerie Thierry Salvador, October 25–November 22, 1990).

31. Professor Wilhelm Weber's account of Schneider's friendship with Picasso (see www.franz-schnei.de, consulted November 16, 2016) may well have come from their mutual friend D.-H. Kahnweiler.

32. My thanks to Anne-Françoise Gavanon for generously providing me with background information on Arnéra and his working techniques in linocut.

33. Sandra Benedretti-Pellard, "Entretien avec Hidalgo Arnéra," in *Picasso à Vallauris: Linogravures*, exh. cat. (Vallauris: Musée national Picasso-Paris, *La Guerre et la Paix*; Musée Magnelli, Musée de la Céramique; June 16–November 19, 2001), 17.

34. Brigitte Baer, *Picasso Peintre-Graveur*, vol. 4 (Bern: Kornfeld, 1988), 396.

35. Pietro Citati, "En Souvenir de Piero Crommelynck," in *Picasso, Piero Crommelynck: Dialogues d'atelier*, exh. cat. (Paris: Musée de la Vie Romantique, February 28–June 11, 2006), 60.

36. Years later (in 1968), Aldo and Piero Crommelynck would publish a special edition of their father's 1920 play *Le Cocu magnifique* with twelve illustrations by Picasso.

37. Citati, "En Souvenir de Piero Crommeynck", 71.

38. Picasso to Otero, in Roberto Otero, *Forever Picasso*, trans. Elaine Kerrigan (New York: Abrams, 1974), 170.

39. Baer 1876.

40. Piero Crommelynck, quoted in Ann Hindry, "L'Ami graveur," in *Picasso, Piero Crommelynck*, 99.

41. See Janie Cohen, "Picasso's Dialogue with Rembrandt's Art," in *Etched on Memory: The Presence of Rembrandt in the Prints of Goya and Picasso*," exh. cat. (Amsterdam: The Rembrandt House Museum, 2000), 107.

42. Mourlot, *Gravés dans ma mémoire*, 222.

43. Edward Quinn, in conversation with the author, 1983.

CATALOGUE

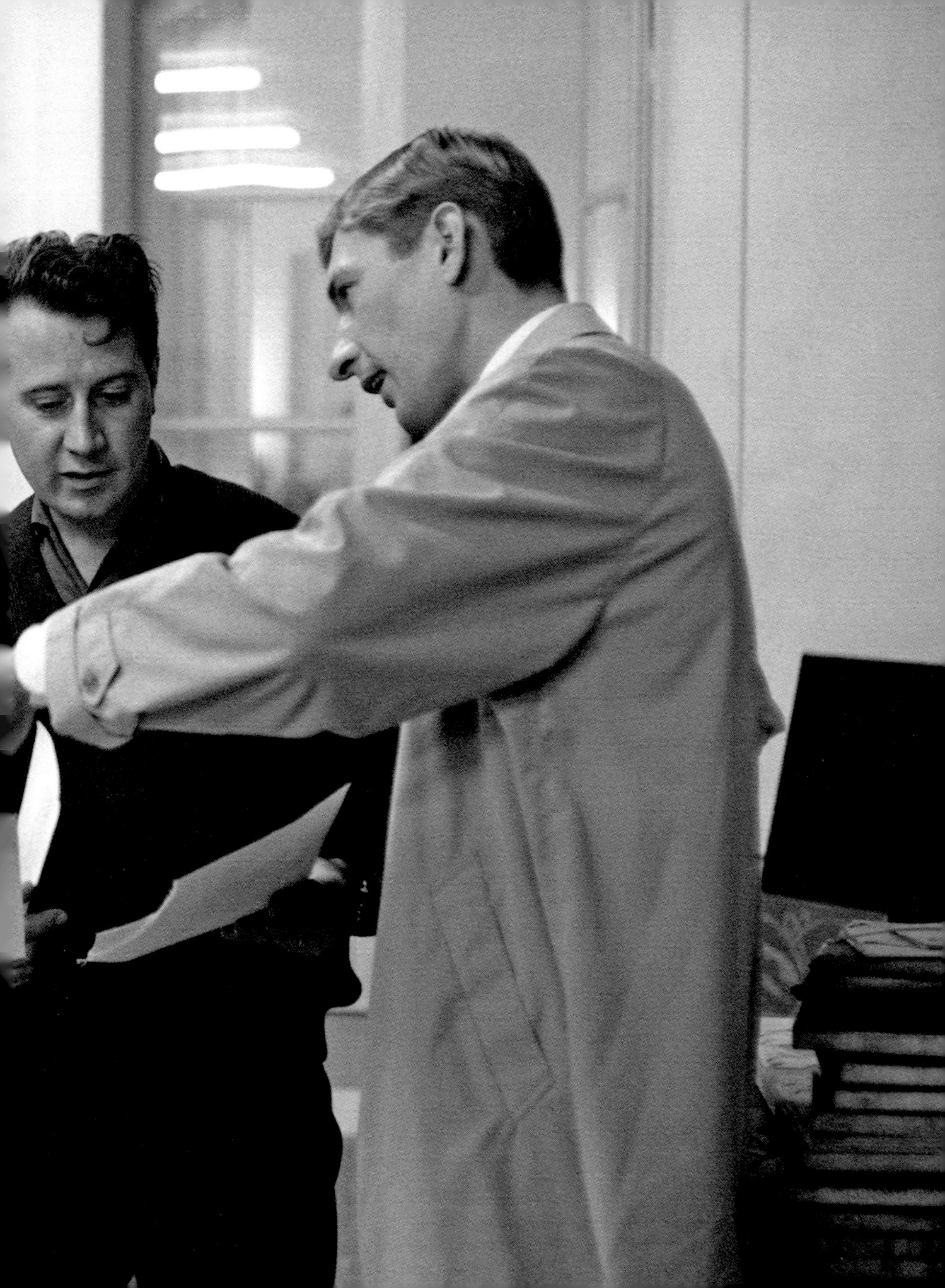

1.

Self-Portrait
Late 1901
Oil on canvas
31 ⅞ × 23 ⅝ in. (81 × 60 cm)
Musée national Picasso-Paris
Pablo Picasso acceptance in lieu,
1979, MP4

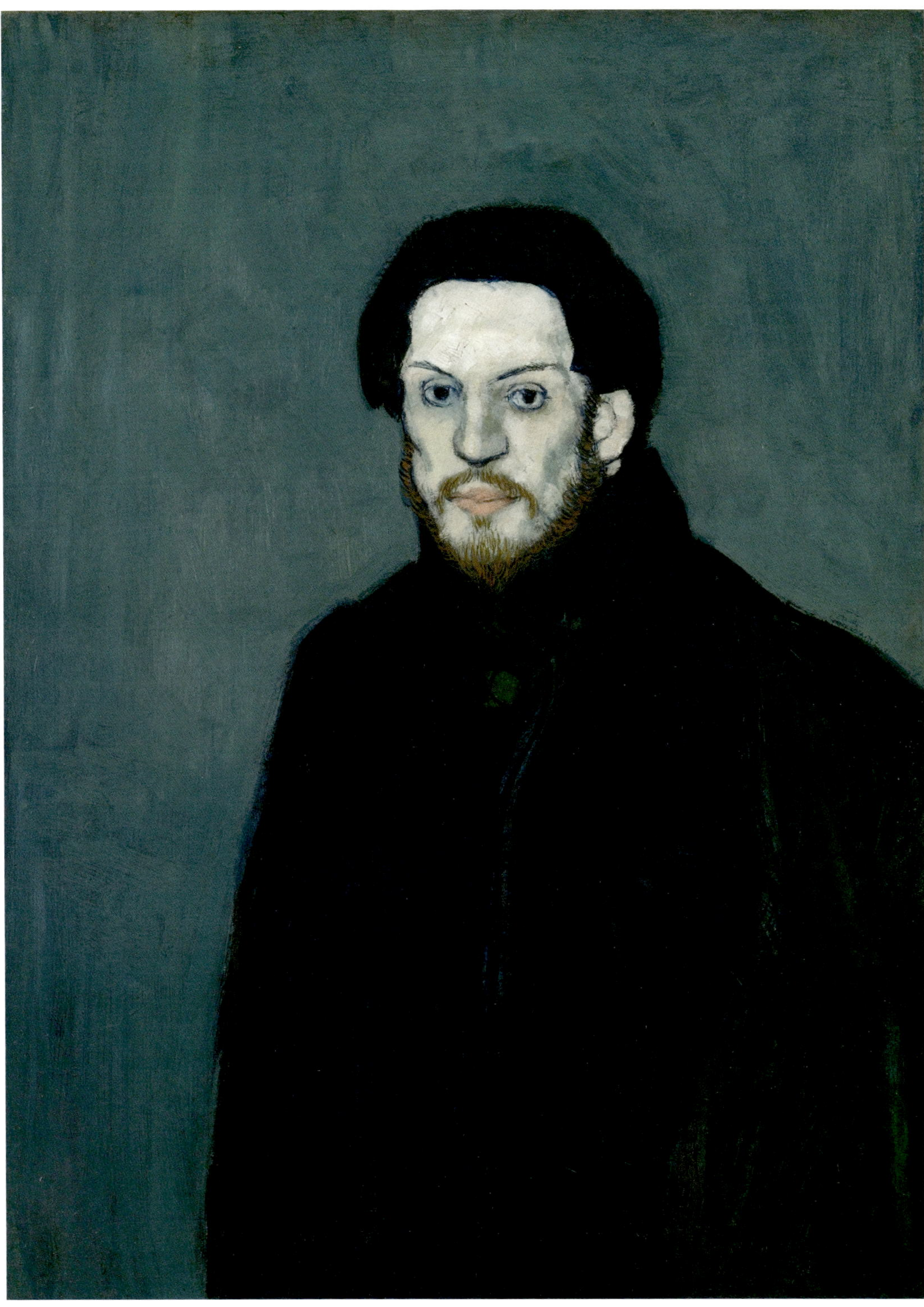

2.
The Frugal Repast
1904
Etching on paper
Plate: 18 ⅛ × 14 ⅞ in. (46.1 ×
37.8 cm); sheet: 20 ¹⁵/₁₆ × 17 ⁷/₁₆ in.
(53.2 × 44.3 cm)
Clark Art Institute

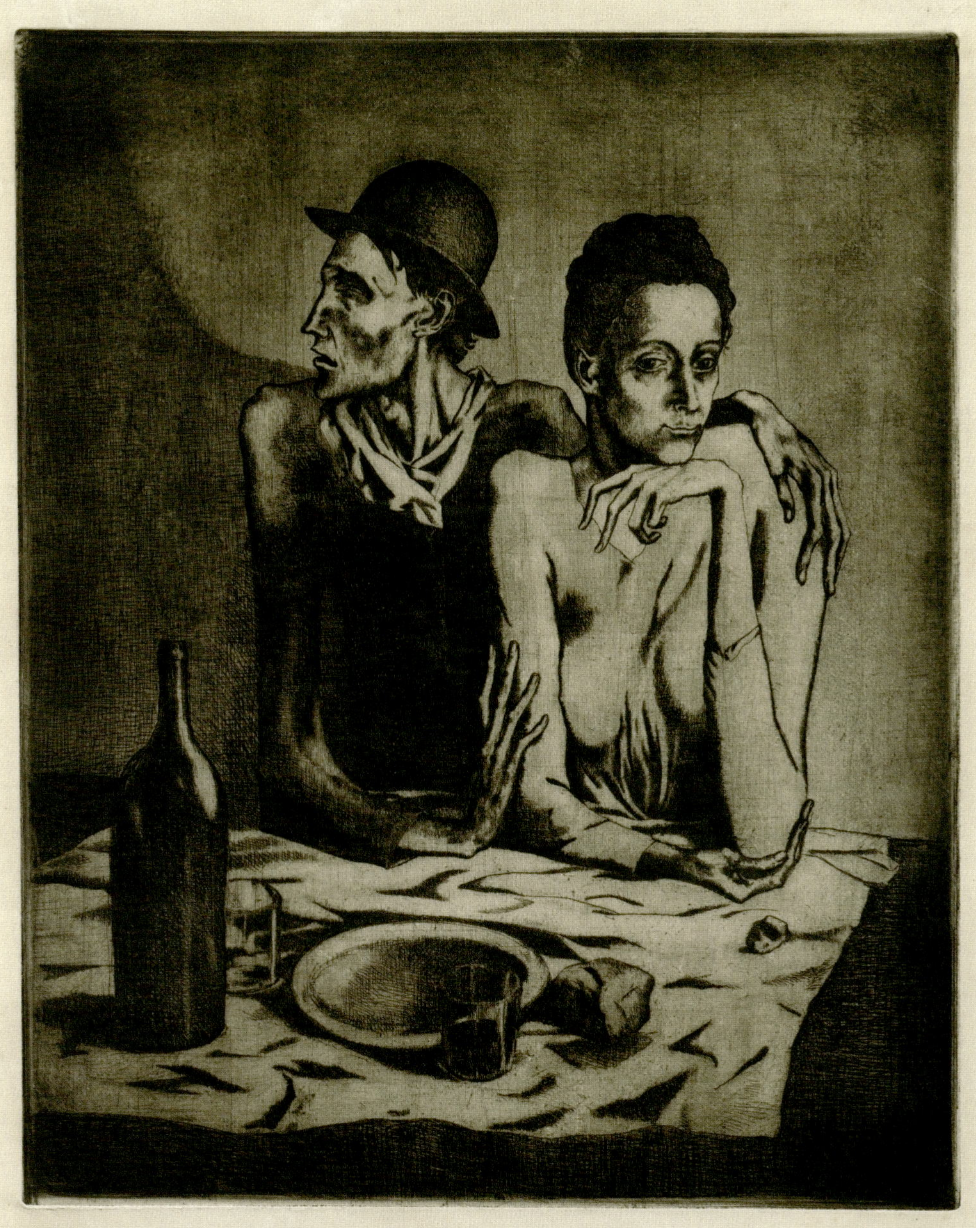

N° 4

Picasso

3.
Salomé, from *The Suite of
the Saltimbanques*
1905
Drypoint on paper
Image: 15 ⅞ × 13 ¾ in. (40.3 ×
34.9 cm); sheet: 25 ⅜ × 19 ⅜ in.
(64.5 × 49.2 cm)
John Szoke Gallery, New York

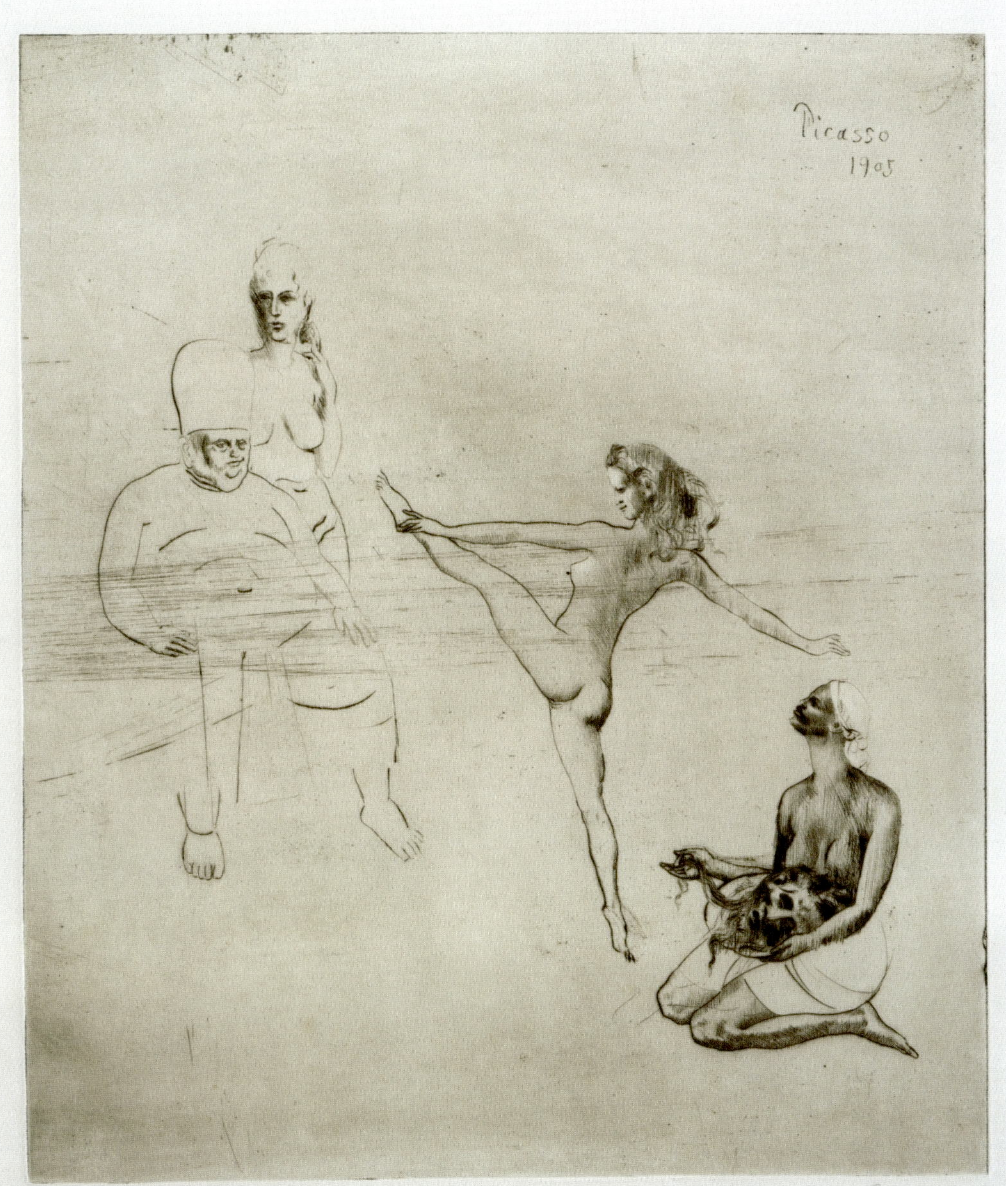

4.
Bust of a Young Woman
(Fernande Olivier)
1906 (printed 1933)
Woodcut on paper
Image and sheet: 19 ¼ × 14 in.
(48.9 × 35.6 cm)
Collection of Catherine Woodard
and Nelson Blitz, Jr.

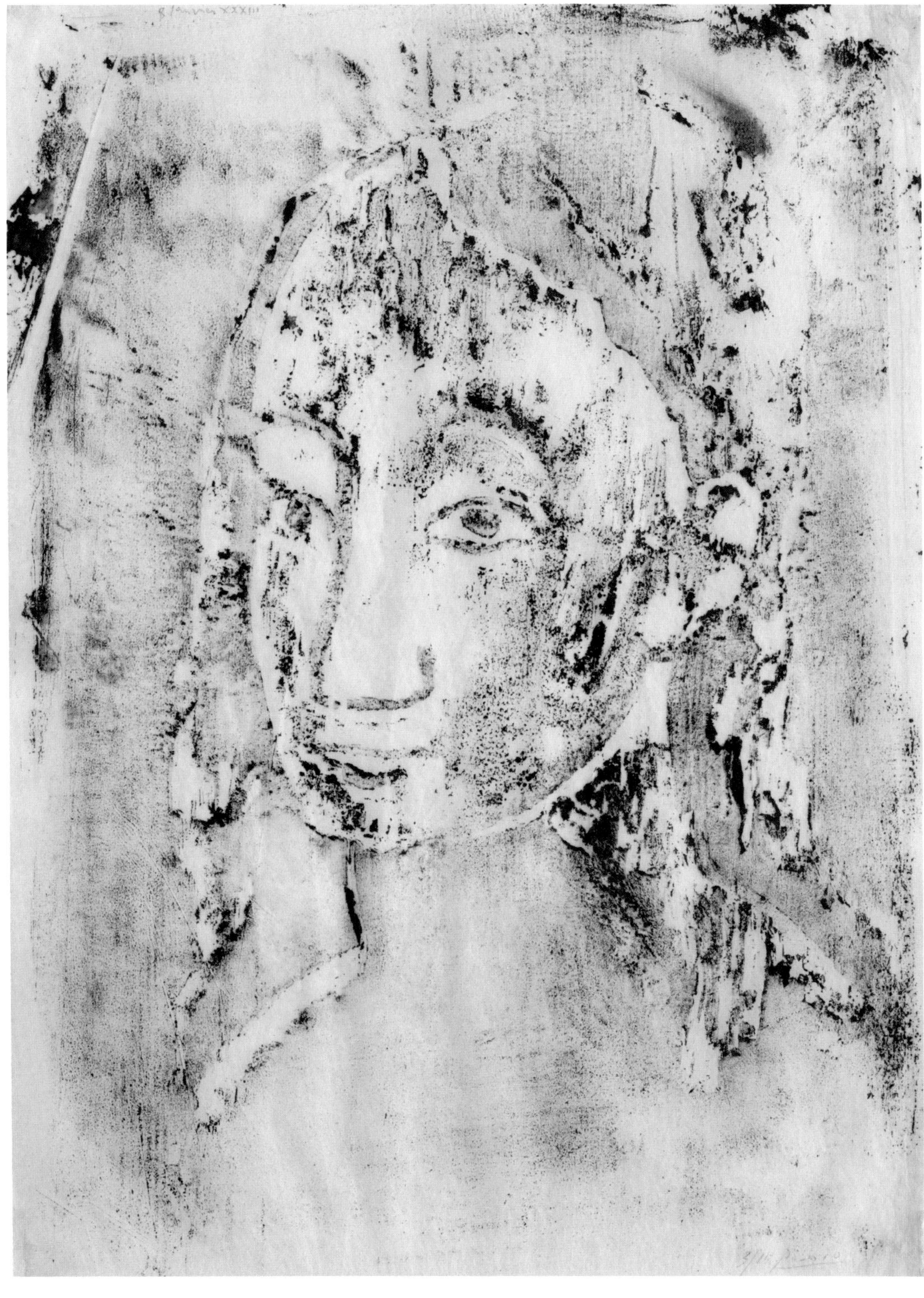

5.
Still Life with Bottle of Marc
1912
Drypoint on paper
Plate: 19 5/8 × 12 in. (49.8 × 30.5 cm);
sheet: 28 3/8 × 21 5/8 in. (72.1 × 54.9 cm)
Philadelphia Museum of Art

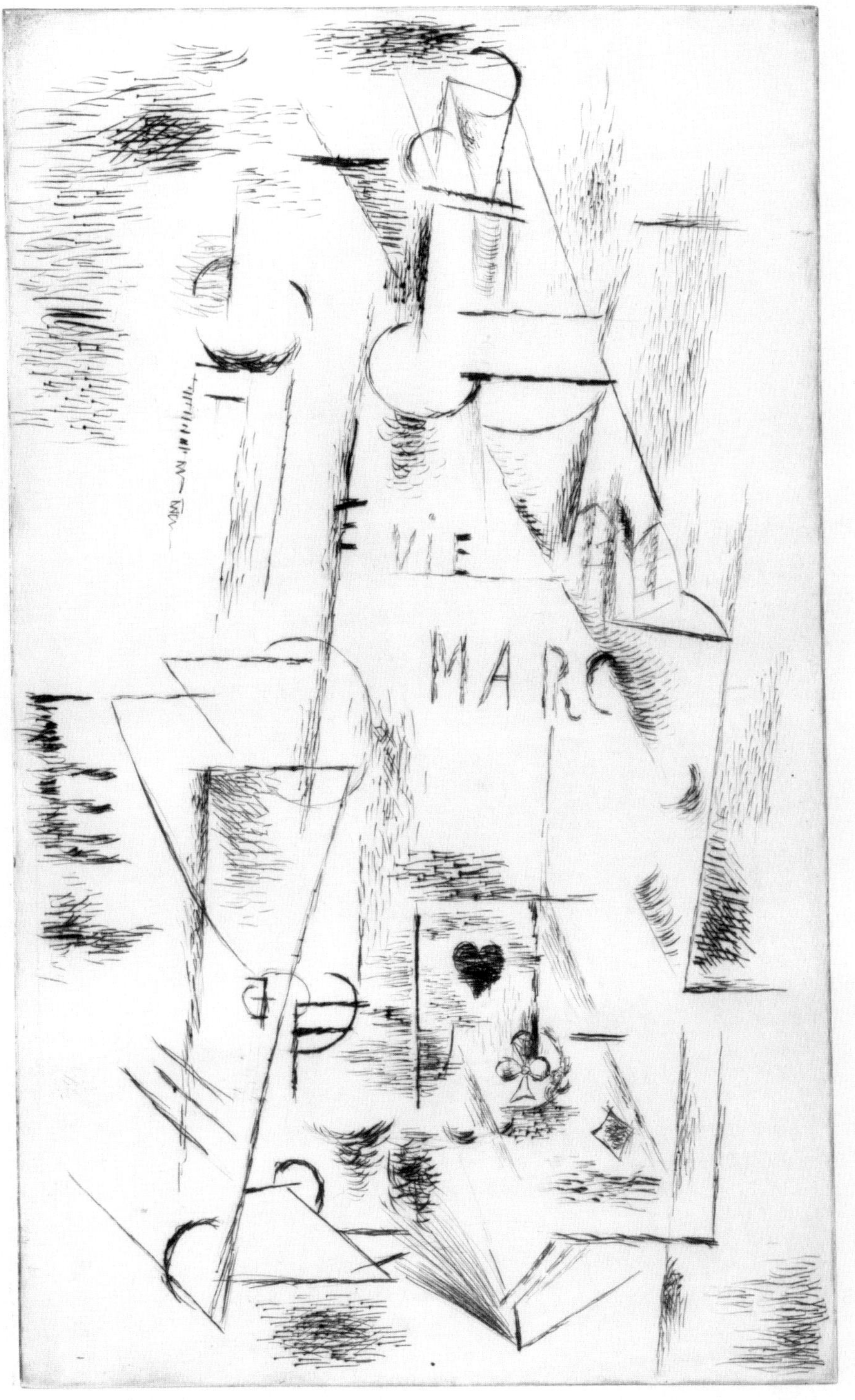
VIE
MARC

6.
Portrait of Olga in a Fur Collar
1923 (printed 1955)
Drypoint on paper
Plate: 19 ½ × 19 ⅜ in. (49.5 × 49.2 cm)
Collection of Catherine Woodard and
Nelson Blitz, Jr.

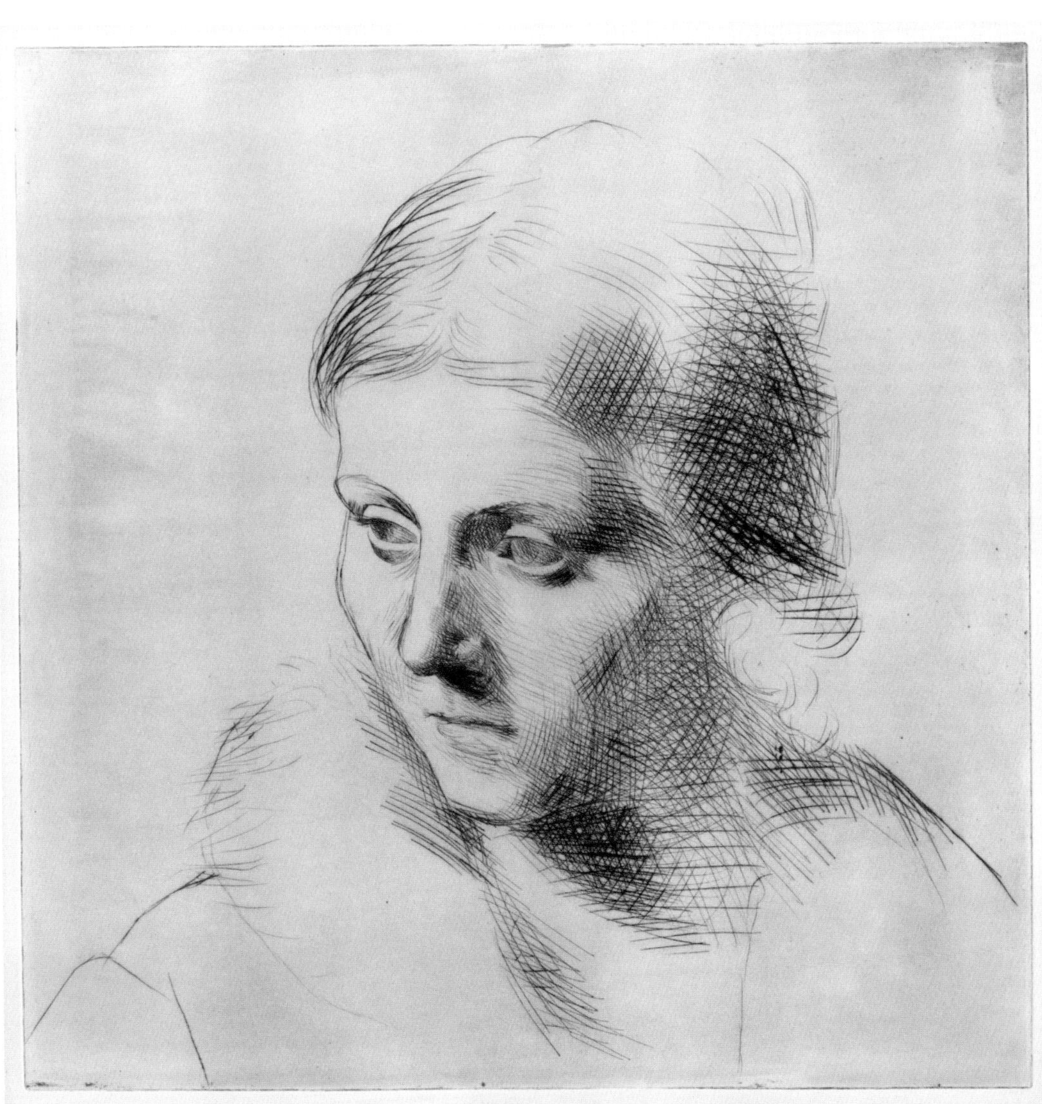

7.
Visage (Face of Marie-Thérèse)
1928
Lithograph on chine collé, laid down
on paper
Image: 8 × 5 ⅝ in. (20.3 × 14.3 cm);
sheet: 10 ¼ × 8 ⅜ in. (26 × 21.3 cm)
John Szoke Gallery, New York

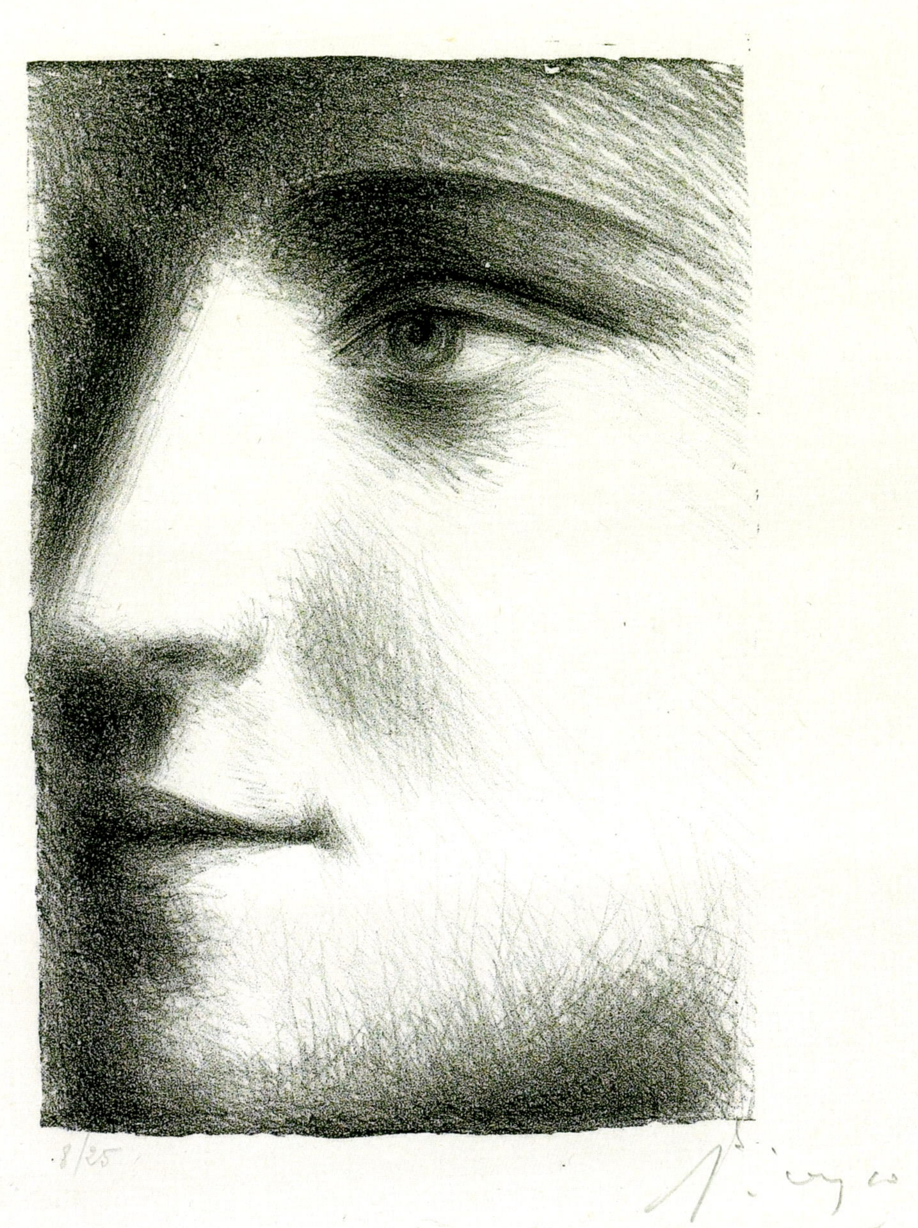
8/25
Picasso

8.
Two Clothed Models, from
The Vollard Suite
1933 (printed 1939)
Etching on paper
Plate: 10 ½ × 7 ⁹⁄₁₆ in. (26.7 ×
19.2 cm); sheet: 17 ½ × 13 ¼ in.
(44.4 × 33.7 cm)
Clark Art Institute

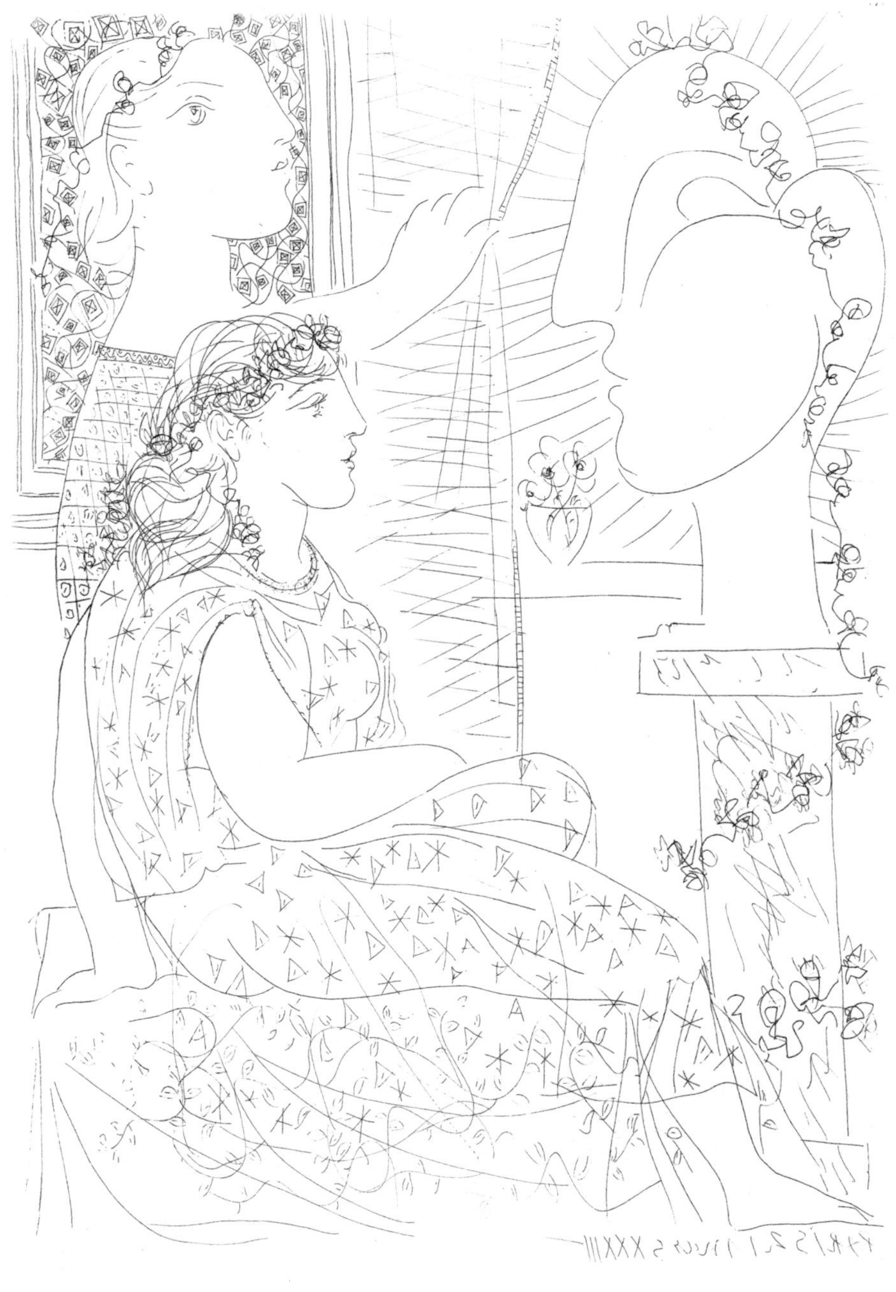

9.
*Large Bullfight, with Female
Bullfighter*
1934 (printed 1939)
Etching on paper
Plate: 19 7/16 × 27 1/16 in. (49.4 ×
68.7 cm); sheet: 22 3/16 × 30 1/4 in.
(56.3 × 76.8 cm)
Museum of Modern Art, New York

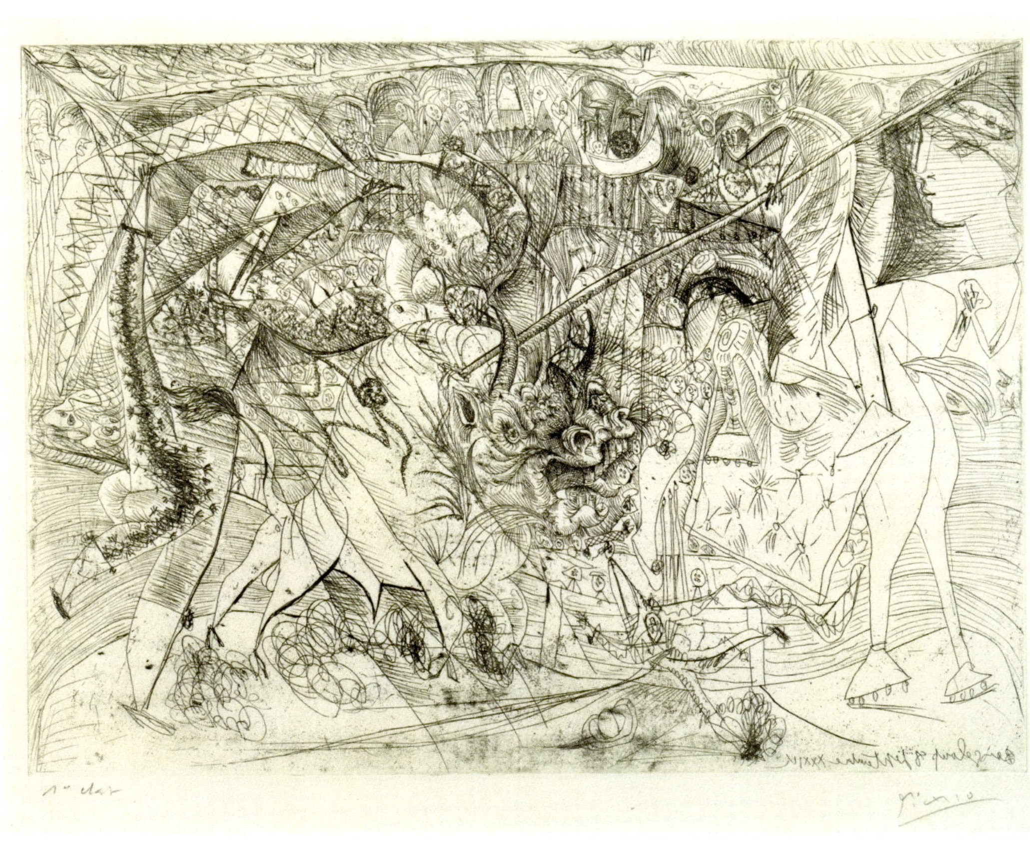

10.
Blind Minotaur Led by a Young Girl
1934
Aquatint, engraving, and drypoint
on paper
Plate: 9 11/16 × 13 11/16 in. (24.6 ×
34.8 cm); sheet: 13 1/8 × 17 1/2 in.
(33.4 × 44.5 cm)
Museum of Fine Arts, Boston
Photograph © 2017 Museum of Fine
Arts, Boston

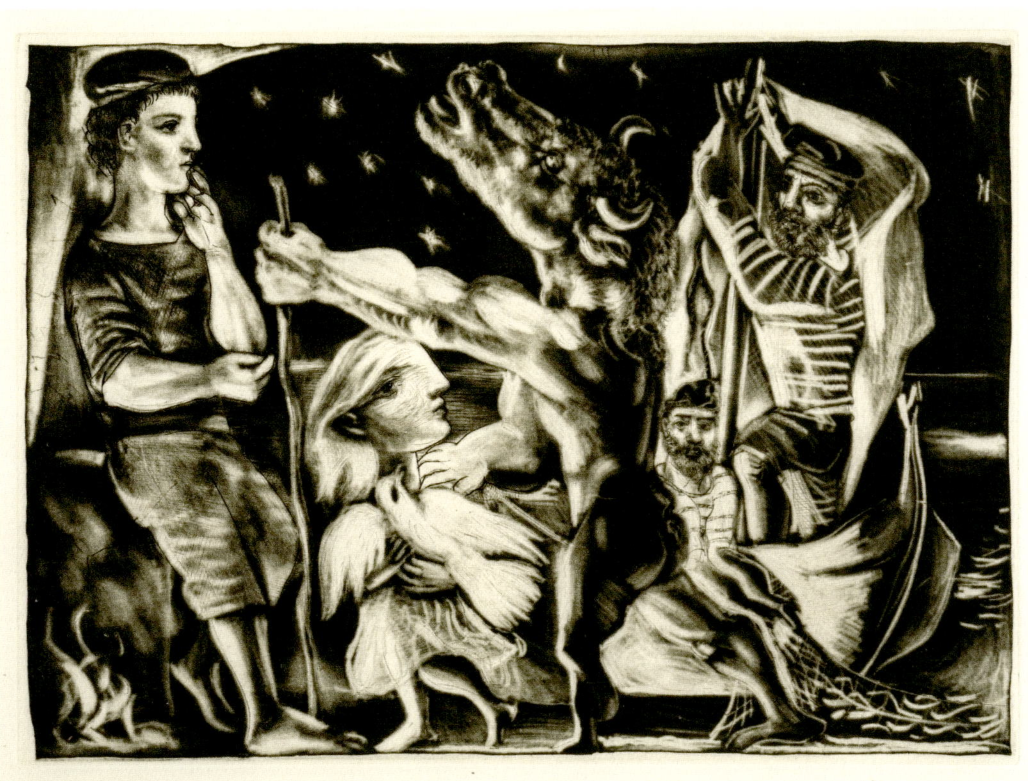

11.
Minotauromachia
1935 (printed 1936)
Etching and engraving on paper
Plate: 19 ½ × 27 ¼ in. (49.5 ×
69.2 cm); sheet: 22 ¼ × 30 in.
(56.5 × 76.2 cm)
Private Collection

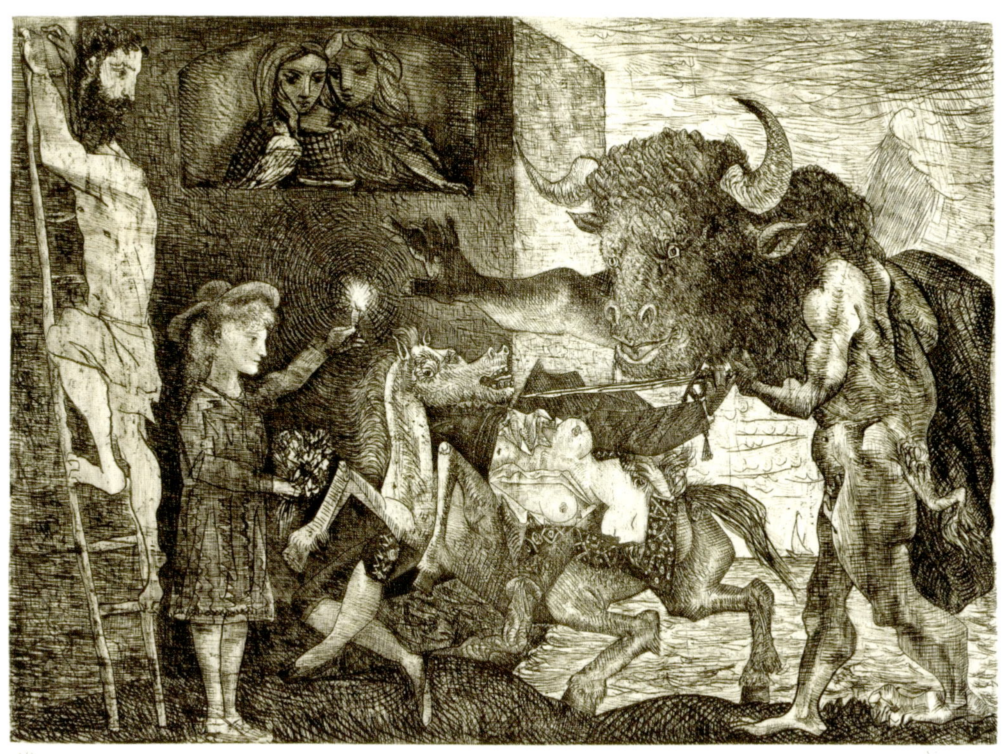

12.
*Faun Unveiling a Sleeping Girl
(Jupiter and Antiope, after
Rembrandt)*, from *The Vollard Suite*
1936 (printed 1939)
Aquatint and sugar-lift aquatint,
engraving, and scraper on paper
Image: 12 ½ × 16 ¼ in. (31.8 ×
41.3 cm); sheet: 15 ¼ × 19 ½ in.
(38.7 × 49.5 cm)
Collection of Catherine Woodard
and Nelson Blitz, Jr.

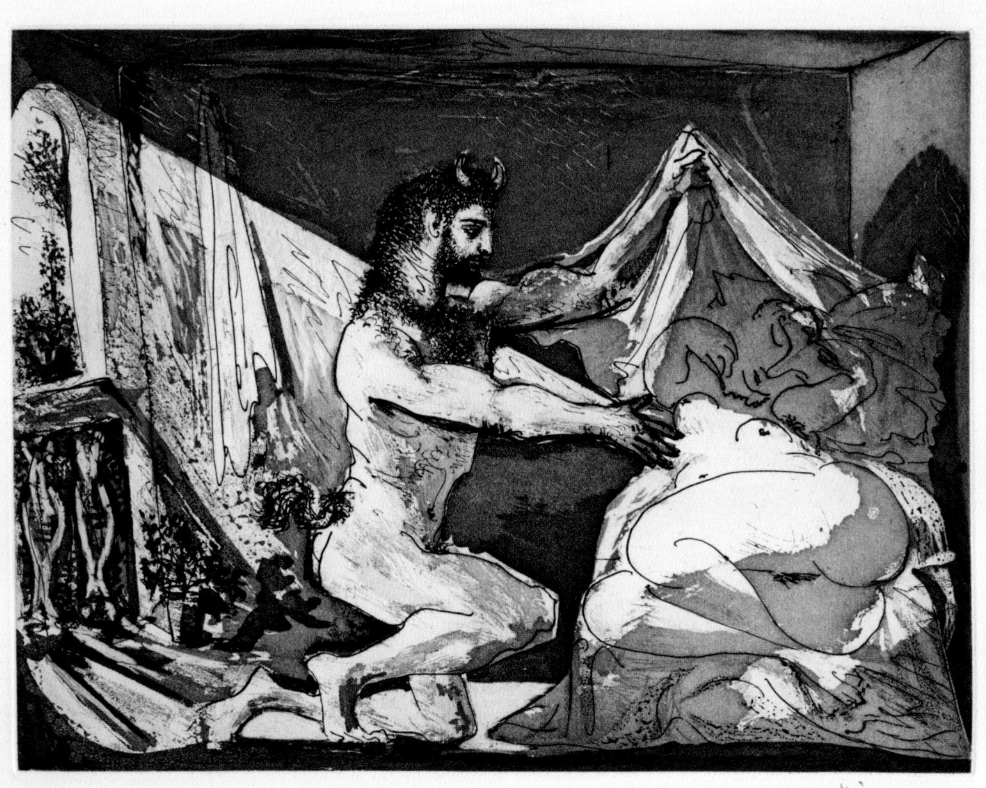

13.
Portrait of Dora Maar
1937
Oil on canvas
36 ¼ × 25 ⅝ in. (92 × 65 cm)
Musée national Picasso-Paris
Pablo Picasso acceptance in lieu,
1979, MP158

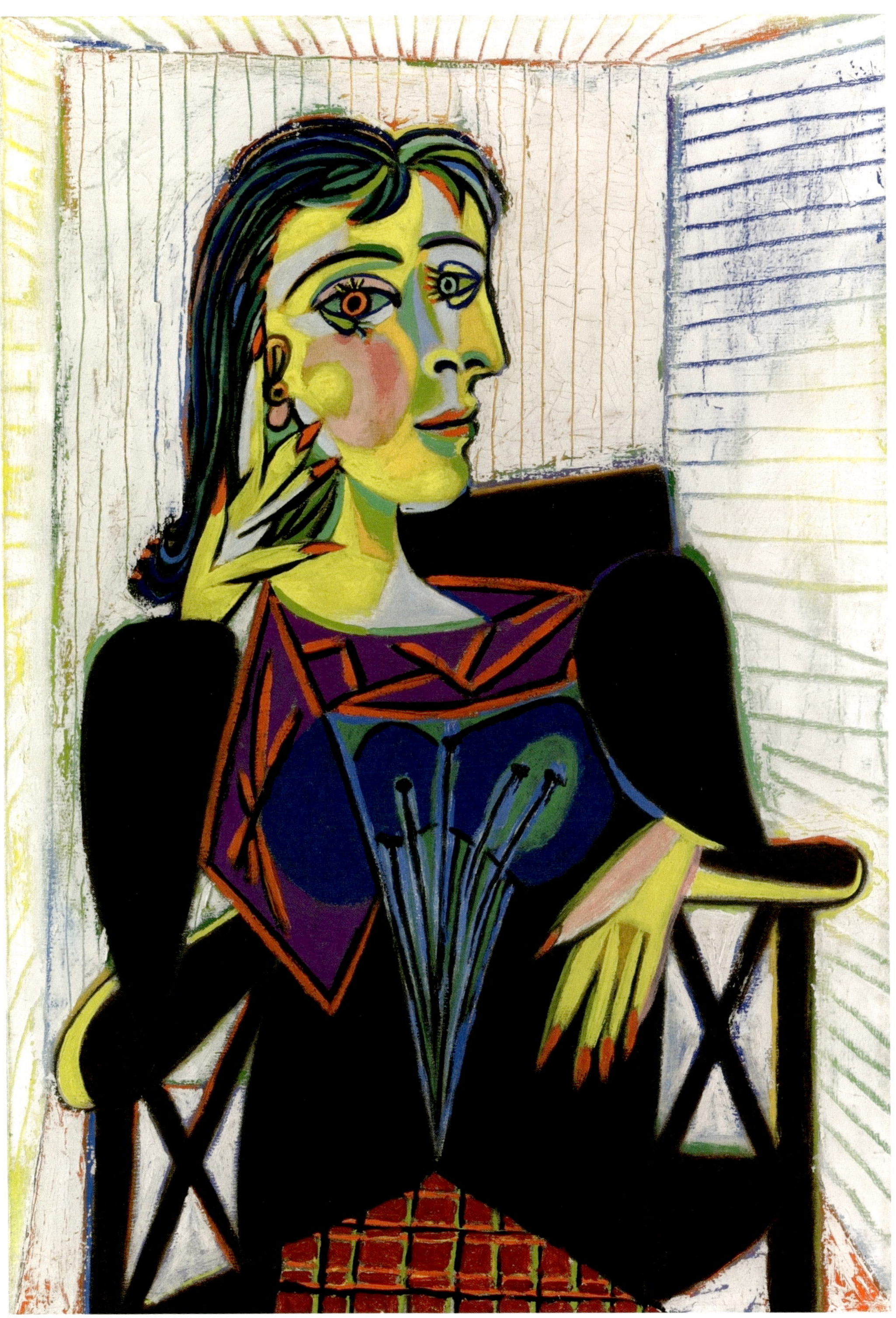

14.
The Weeping Woman, I
1937
Drypoint, aquatint, etching, and
scraper on paper
Plate: 27 ⅛ × 19 ½ in. (68.9 ×
49.5 cm); sheet: 30 5/16 × 22 5/16 in.
(77 × 56.7 cm)
Museum of Modern Art, New York

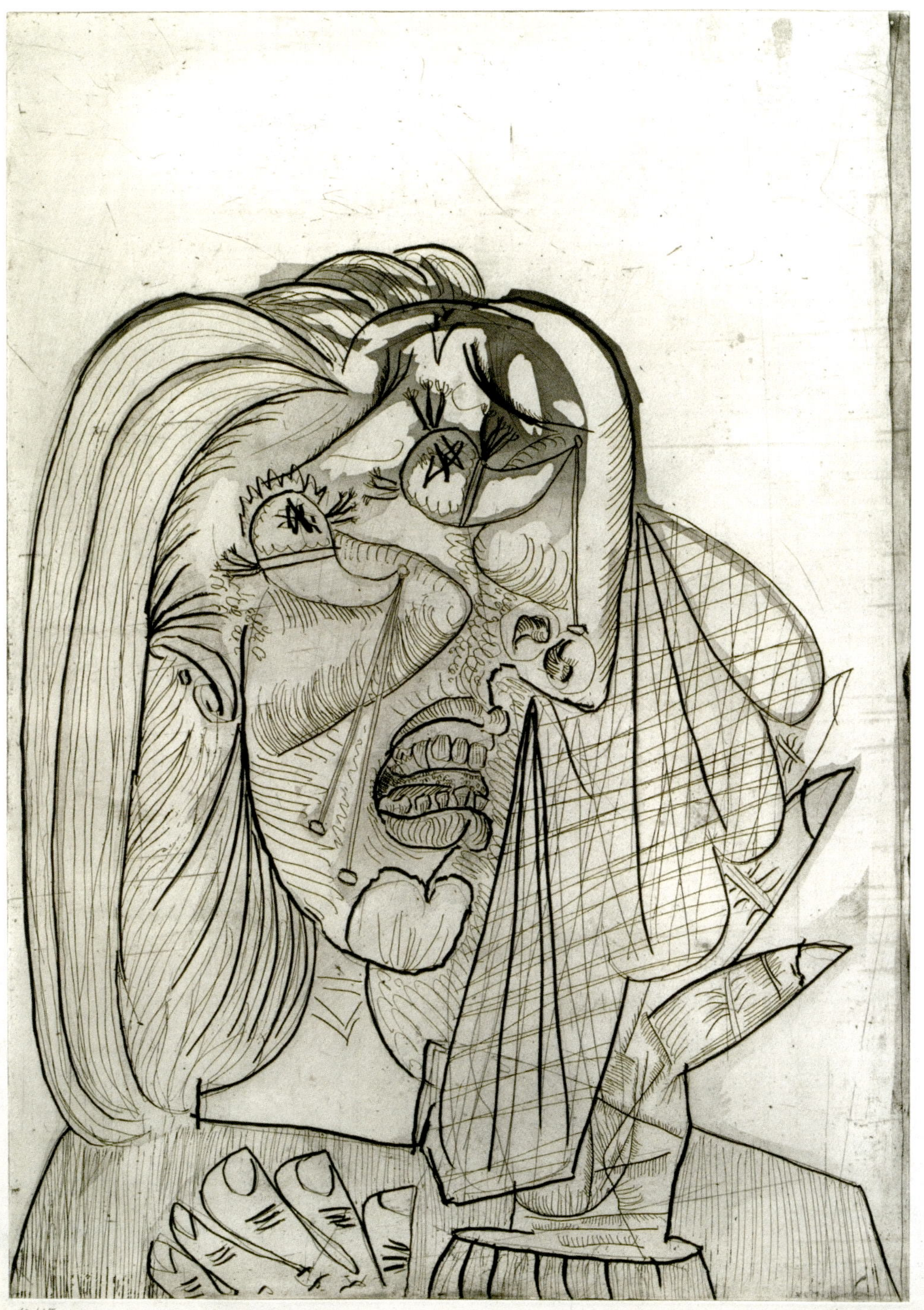

15.
The Weeping Woman, I
1937
Drypoint, aquatint, etching,
and scraper on paper
Image: 27 ⅛ × 19 ⅜ in. (68.9 ×
49.2 cm); sheet: 30 ½ × 25 ⅝ in.
(77.5 × 65.1 cm)
Private Collection

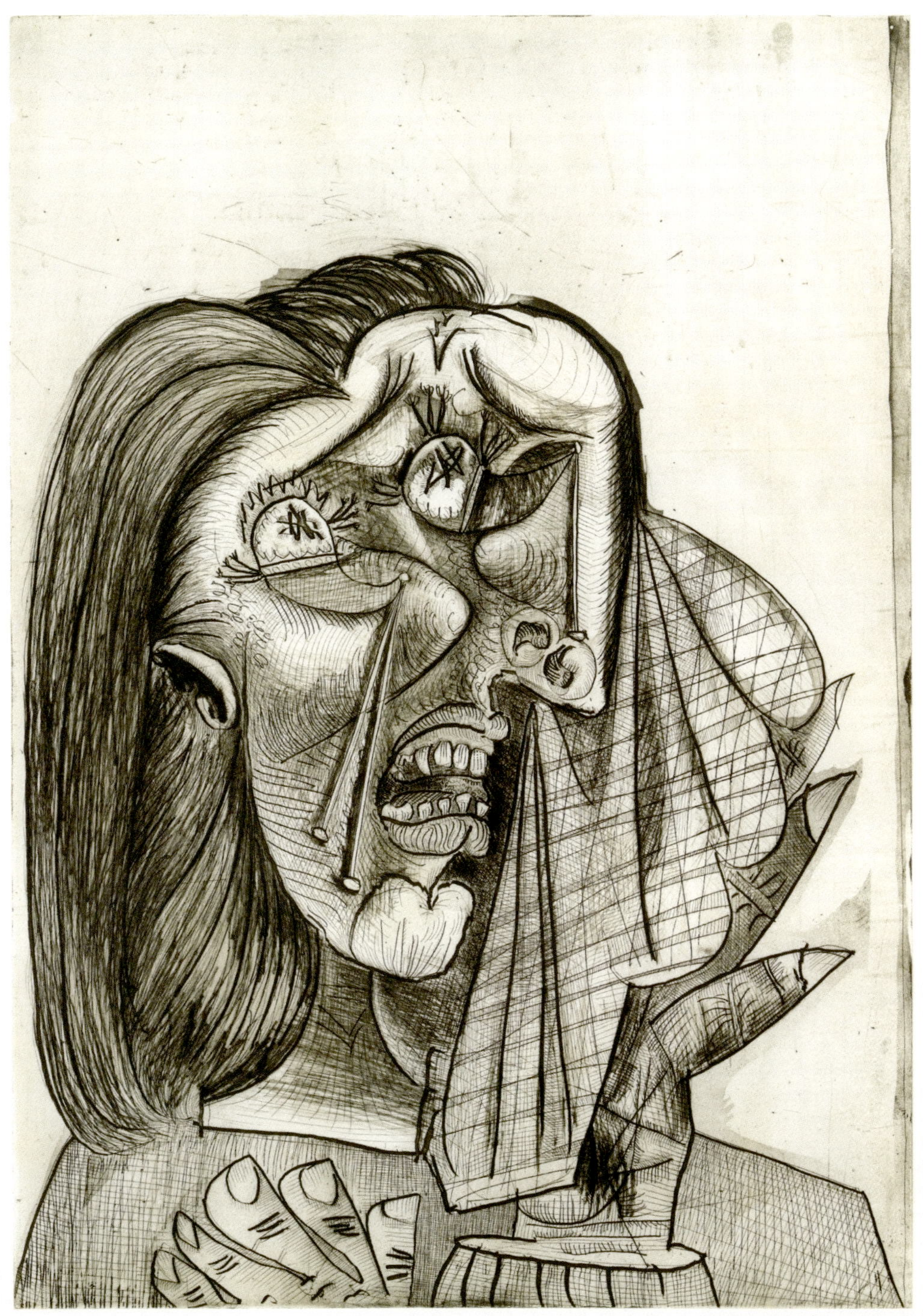

8/15
Picasso

16.
The Weeping Woman, III
1937
Drypoint, aquatint, and foul-biting
on paper
Plate: 13 ⅝ × 9 ⅝ in. (34.6 × 24.6 cm)
Collection of Catherine Woodard
and Nelson Blitz, Jr.

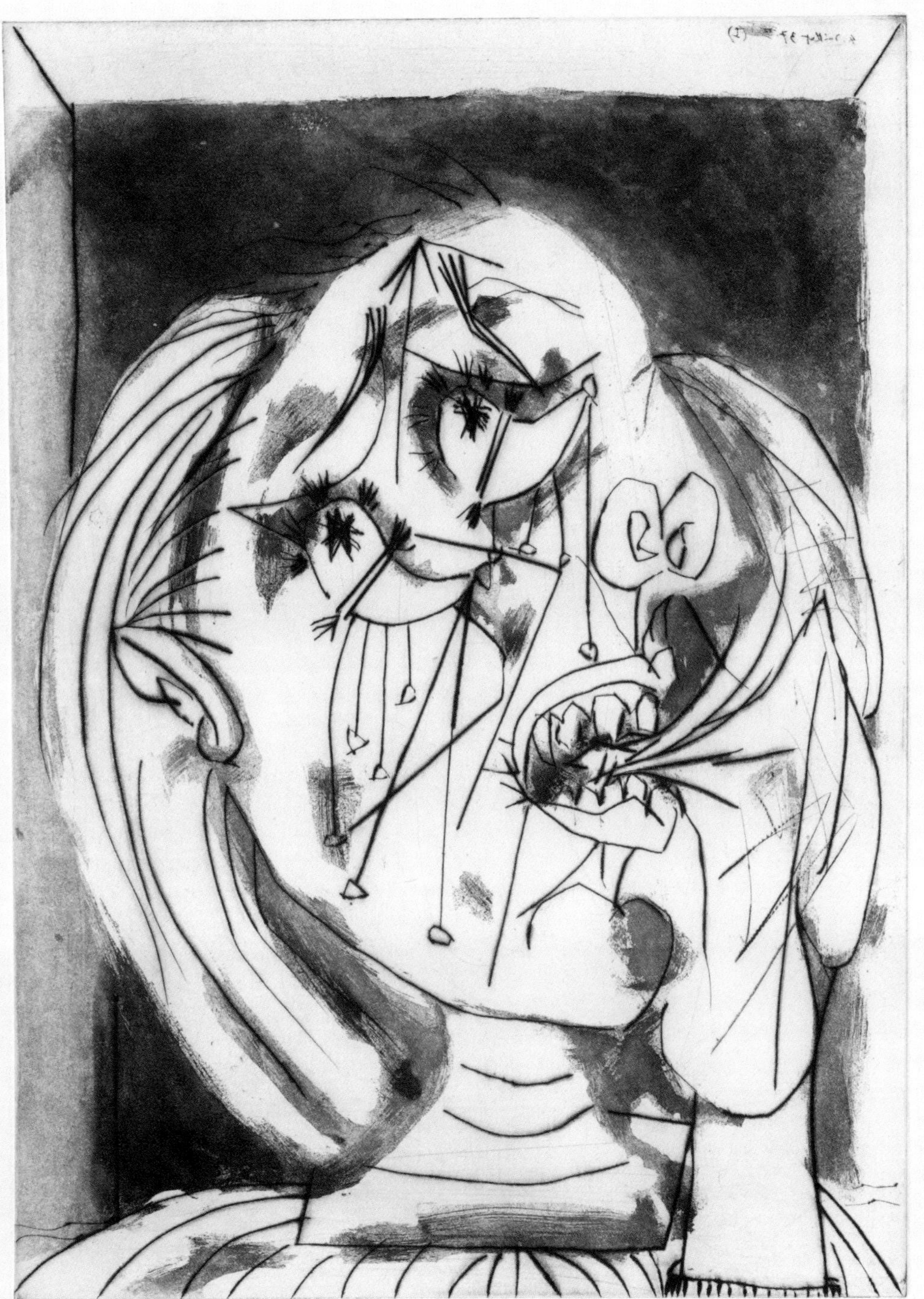

17.
The Weeping Woman, IV
1937
Drypoint on paper
Plate: 13 ⅝ × 9 ⅞ in. (34.7 × 25 cm)
Collection of Catherine Woodard
and Nelson Blitz, Jr.

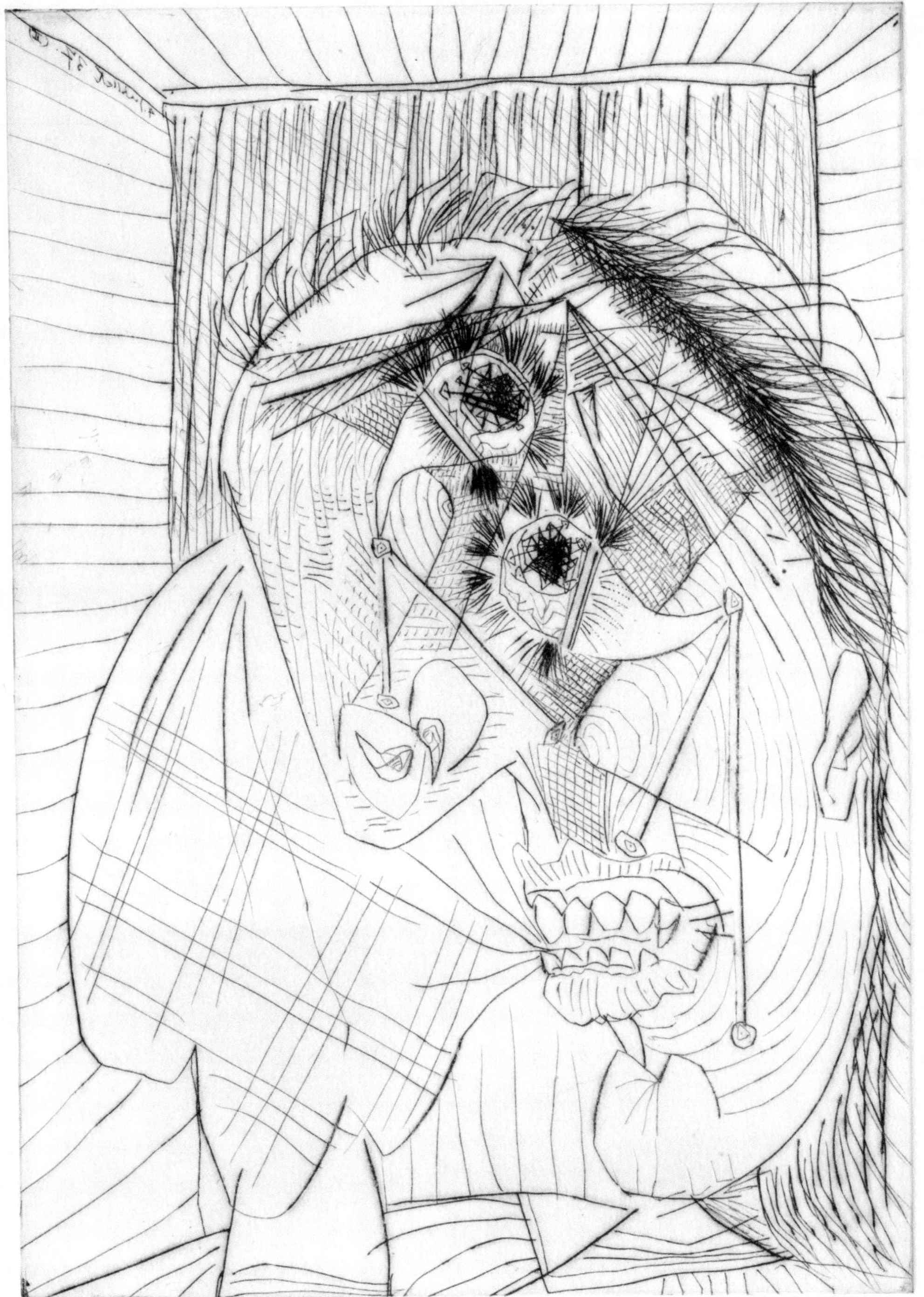

18.
Woman with Tambourine
1939 (printed 1943)
Etching, aquatint, and scraper
on paper
Image: 26 ⅛ × 20 ⅛ in. (66.4 ×
51.1 cm); sheet: 31 × 22 ⅜ in.
(78.7 × 56.8 cm)
Private Collection

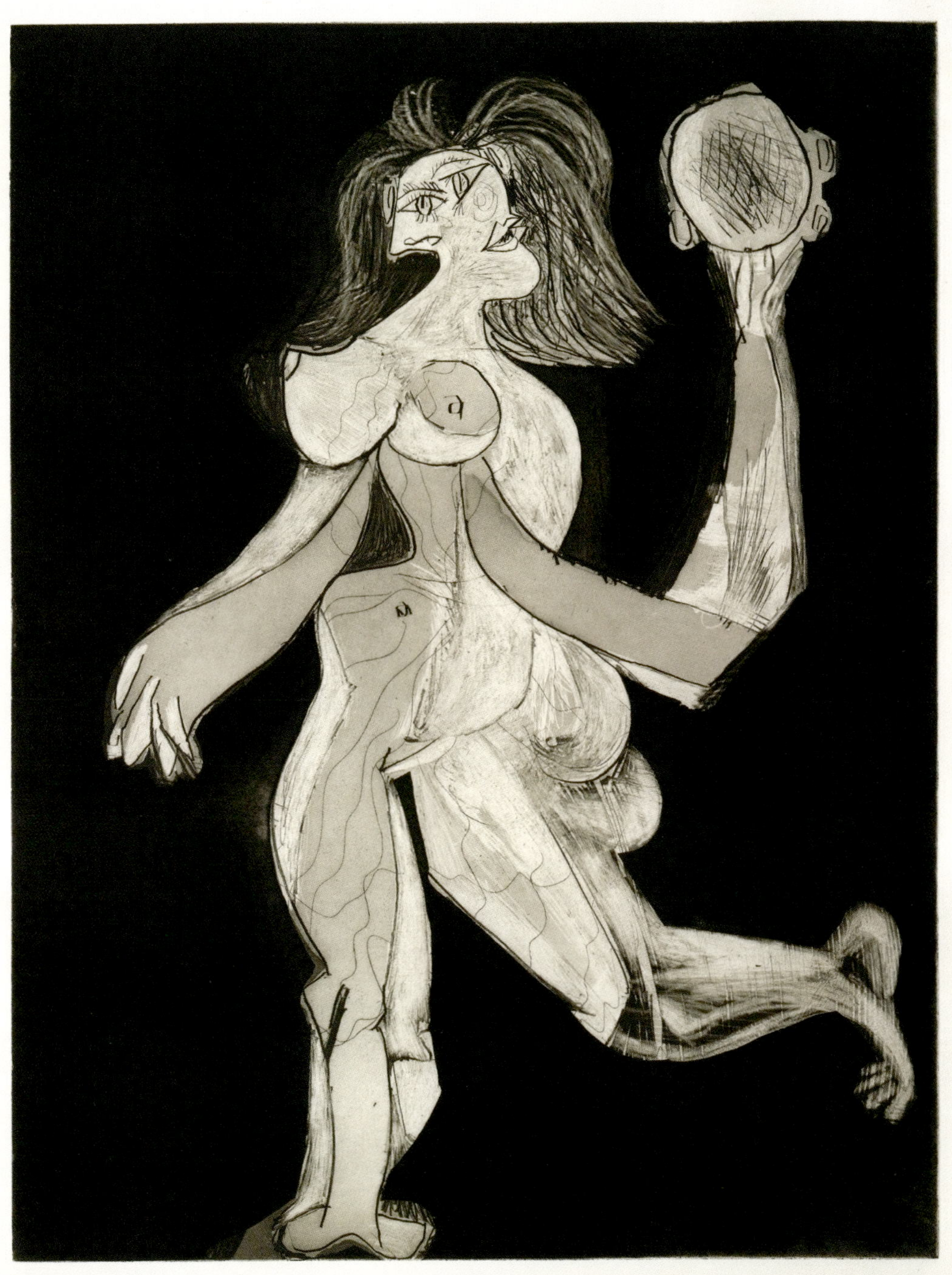

19.
David and Bathsheba
1947
Lithograph printed from zinc plate
on paper
Image: 25 3/16 × 19 5/16 in. (64 × 49 cm);
sheet: 25 7/8 × 19 9/16 in. (65.8 × 49.7 cm)
Museum of Fine Arts, Boston
Photograph © 2017 Museum of Fine
Arts, Boston

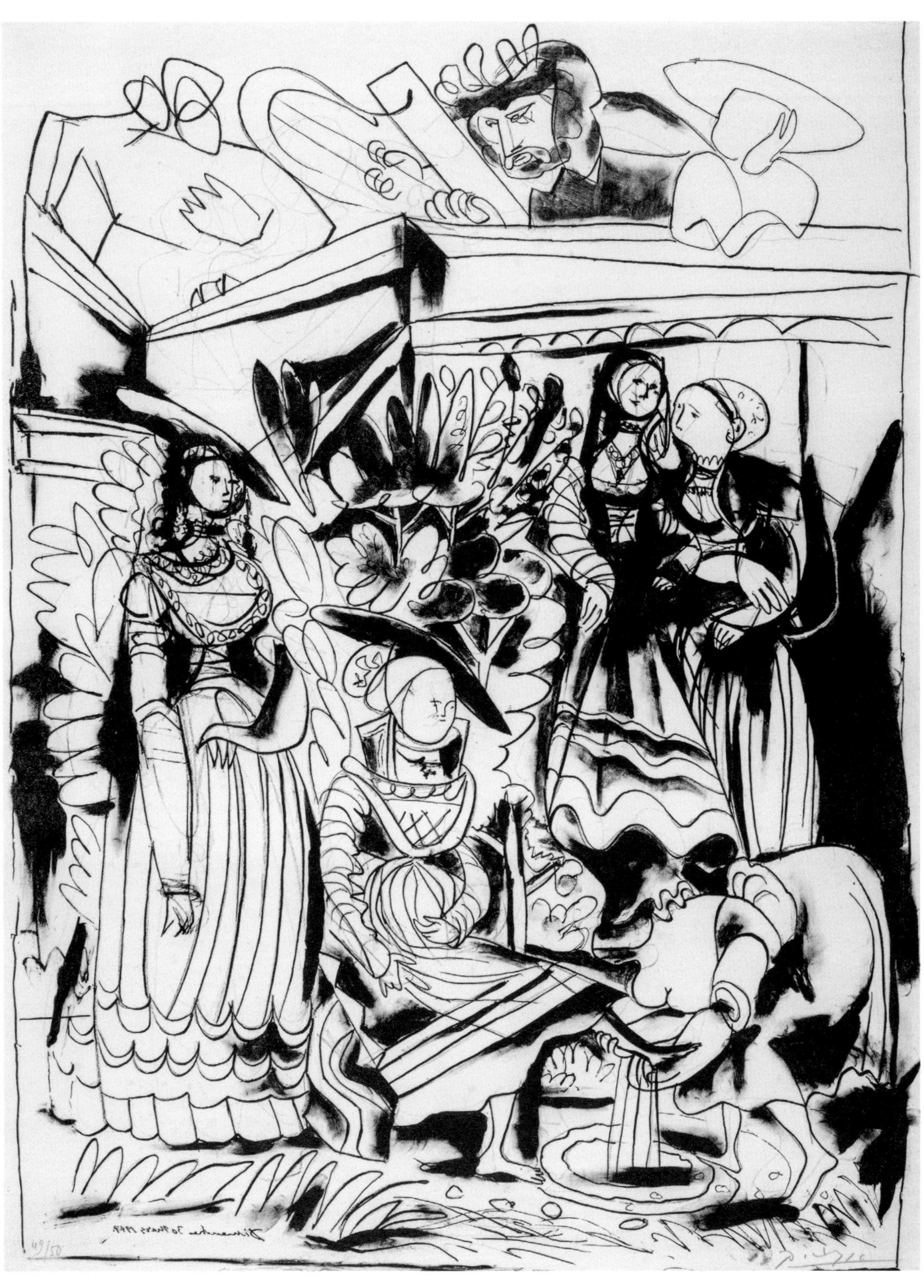

20.
David and Bathsheba
1949
Lithograph on paper
Image: 25 11/16 × 19 1/16 in. (65.3 ×
48.4 cm); sheet: 29 15/16 × 22 in.
(76 × 55.9 cm)
Museum of Fine Arts, Boston
Photograph © 2017 Museum of Fine
Arts, Boston

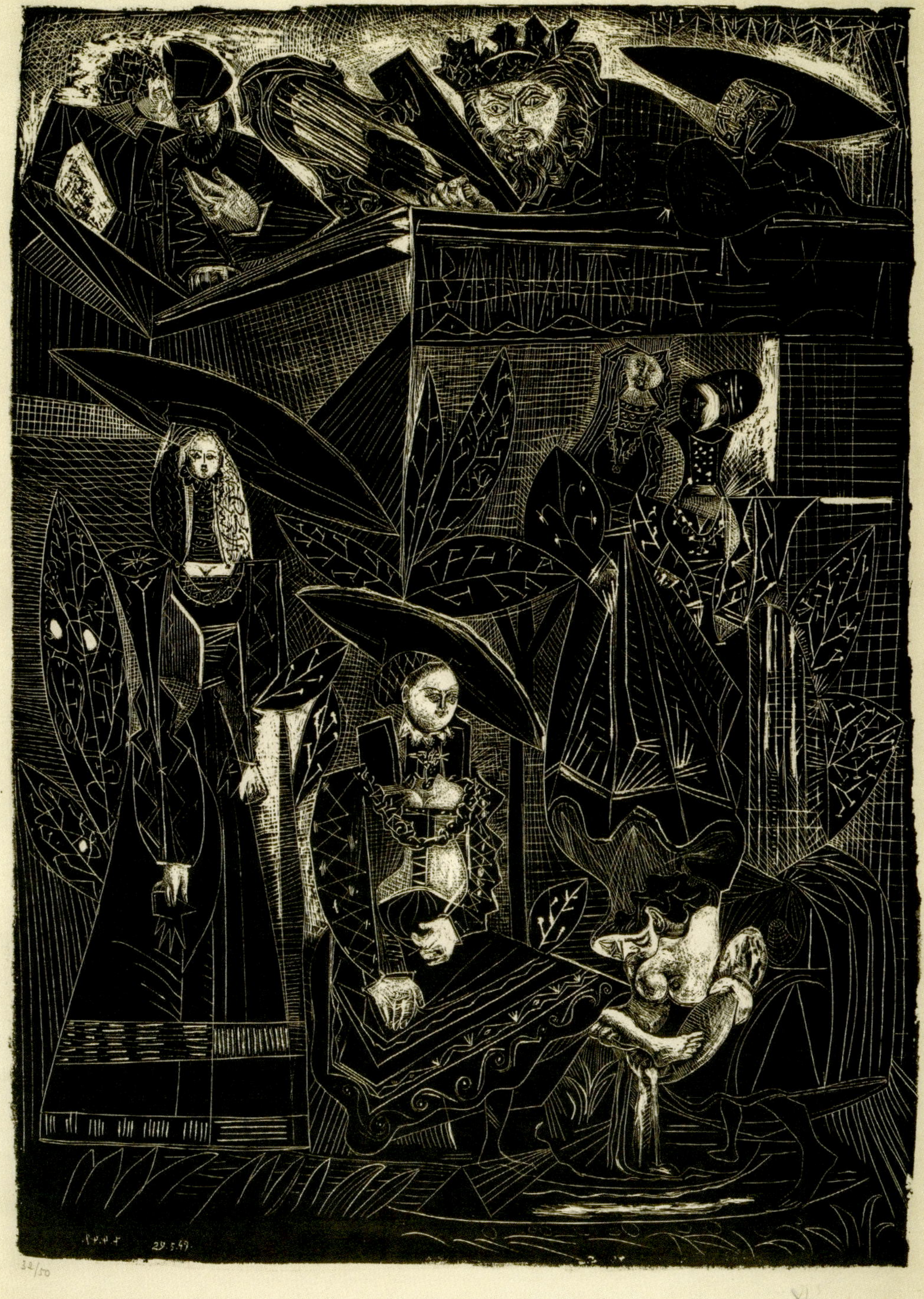

21.
The Dove
1949
Lithograph printed from zinc plate
on paper
Composition: 21 ½ × 27 ⁷⁄₁₆ in.
(54.4 × 70 cm); sheet: 22 × 30 in.
(55.9 × 76.2 cm)
Philadelphia Museum of Art

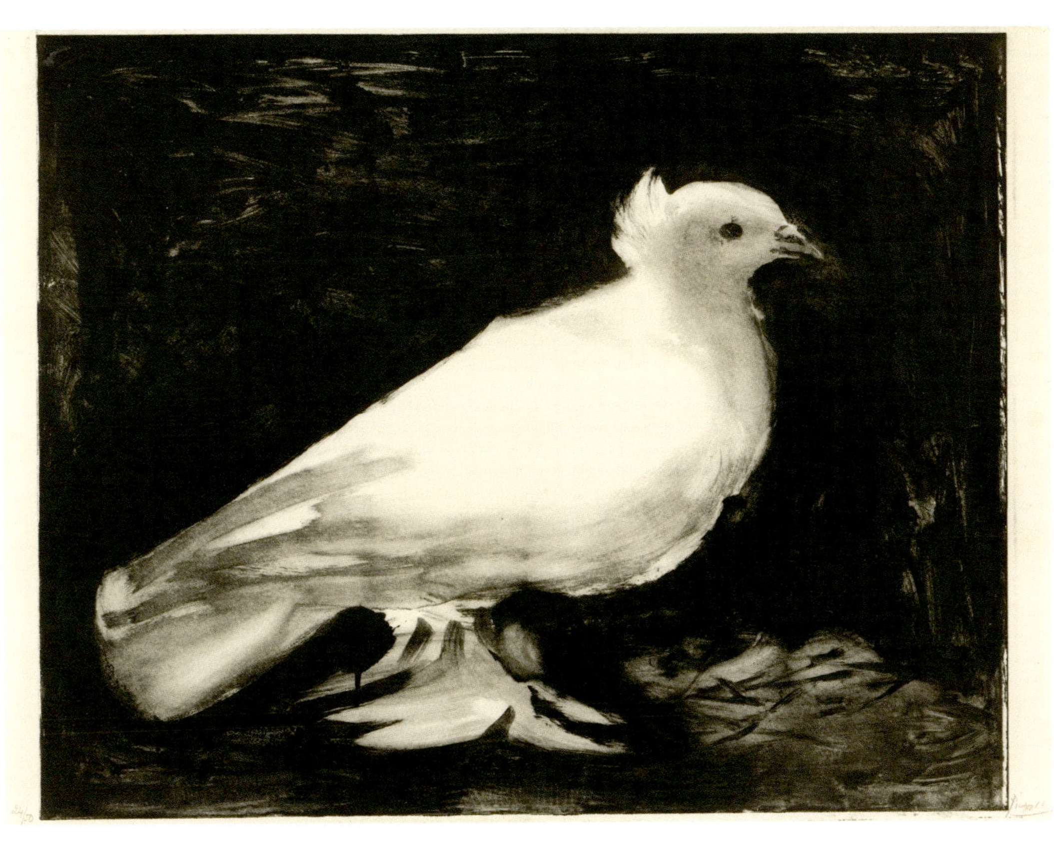

22.
Venus and Cupid, after Cranach
1949 and 1951
Aquatint, scraper, burin and drypoint
on paper
Image: 31 ⅜ × 16 ⅞ in. (79.7 ×
42.9 cm); sheet: 35 ½ × 25 in.
(90.2 × 63.5 cm)
John Szoke Gallery, New York

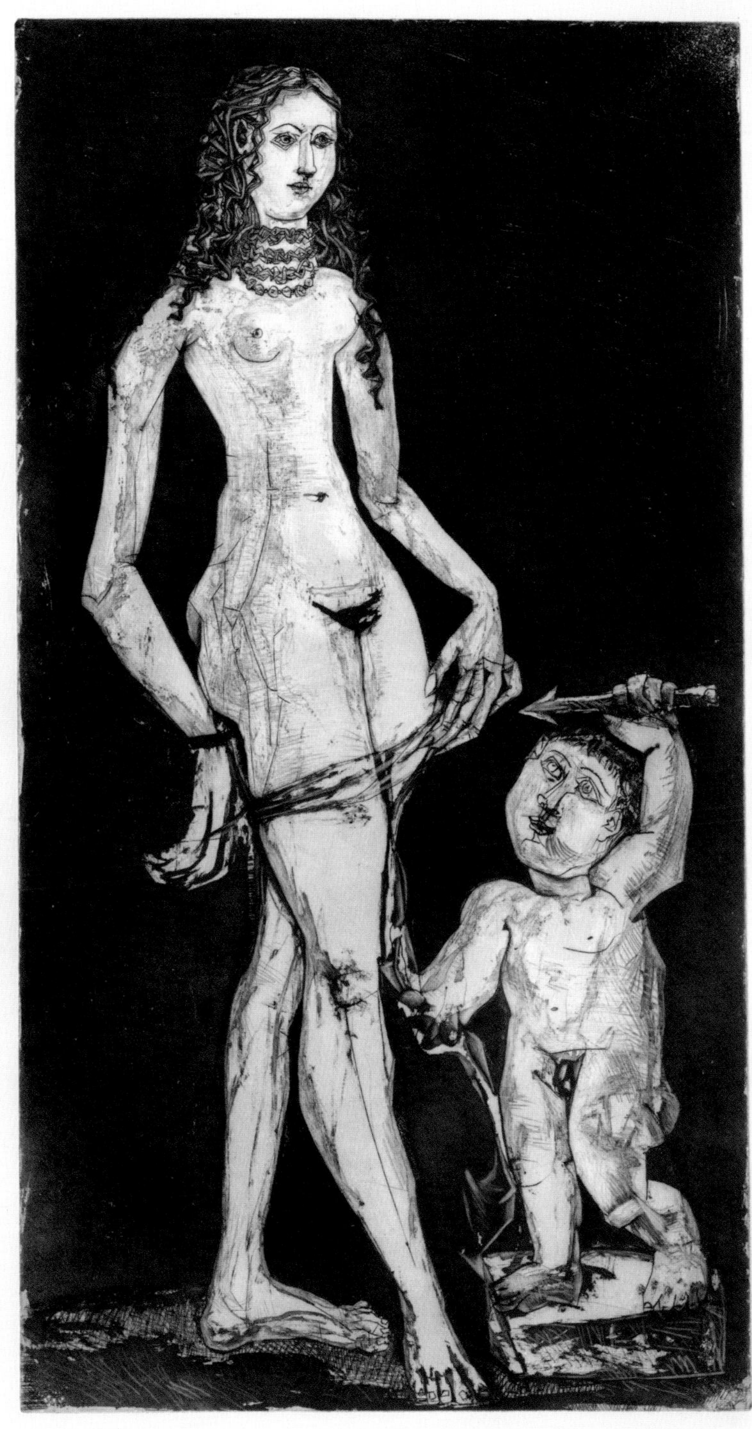

23.
Woman at the Window
1952
Sugar-lift aquatint on paper
Plate: 32 7/8 × 18 5/8 in. (83.5 × 47.3 cm)
Collection of Catherine Woodard
and Nelson Blitz, Jr.

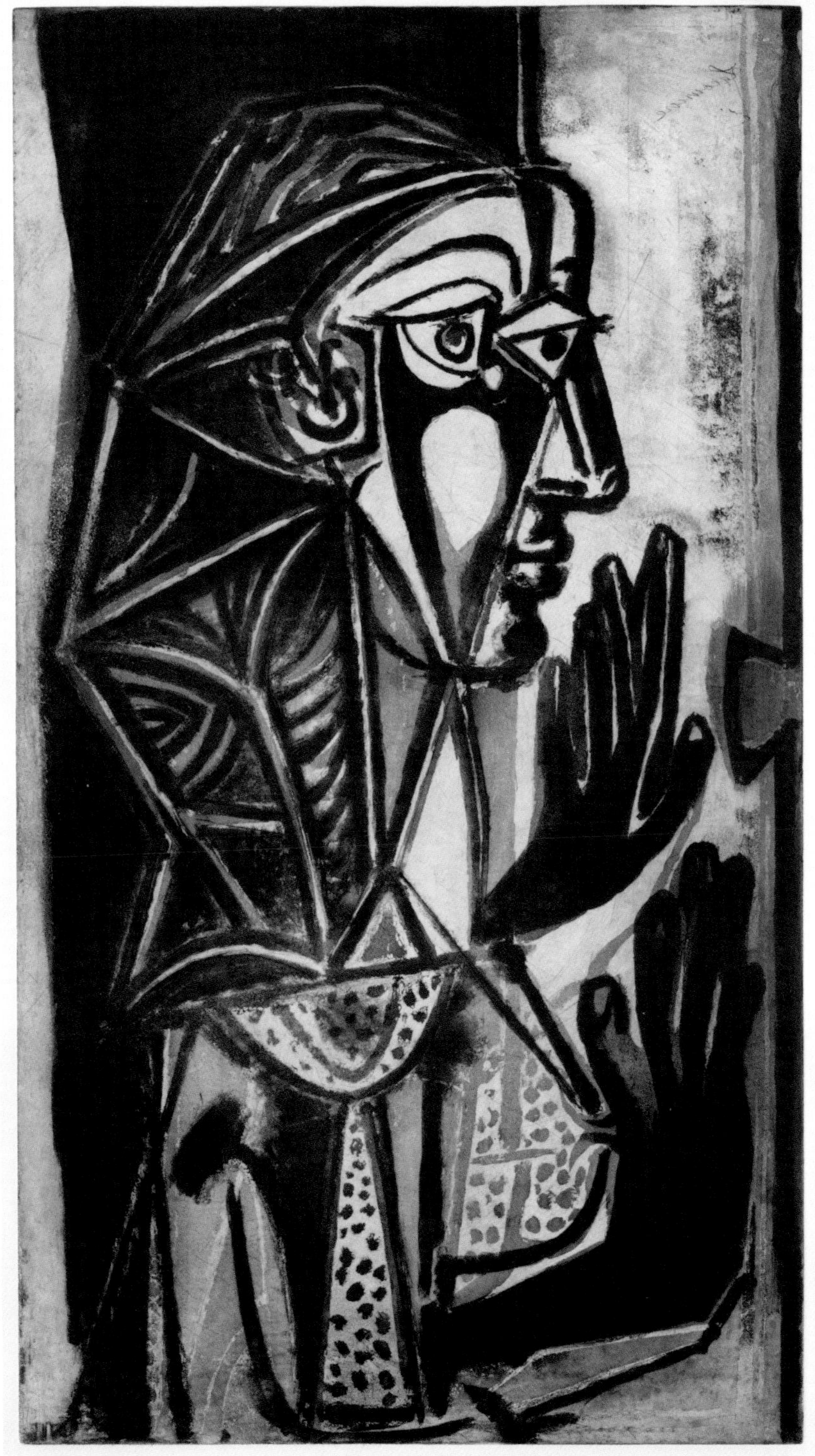

24.
*Paloma and Her Doll on Black
Background*
1952
Lithograph printed from zinc plate
on paper
Composition: 27 11/16 × 21 3/4 in.
(70.4 × 55.3 cm); sheet: 29 1/2 × 22 3/16 in.
(75 × 56.3 cm)
Museum of Modern Art, New York

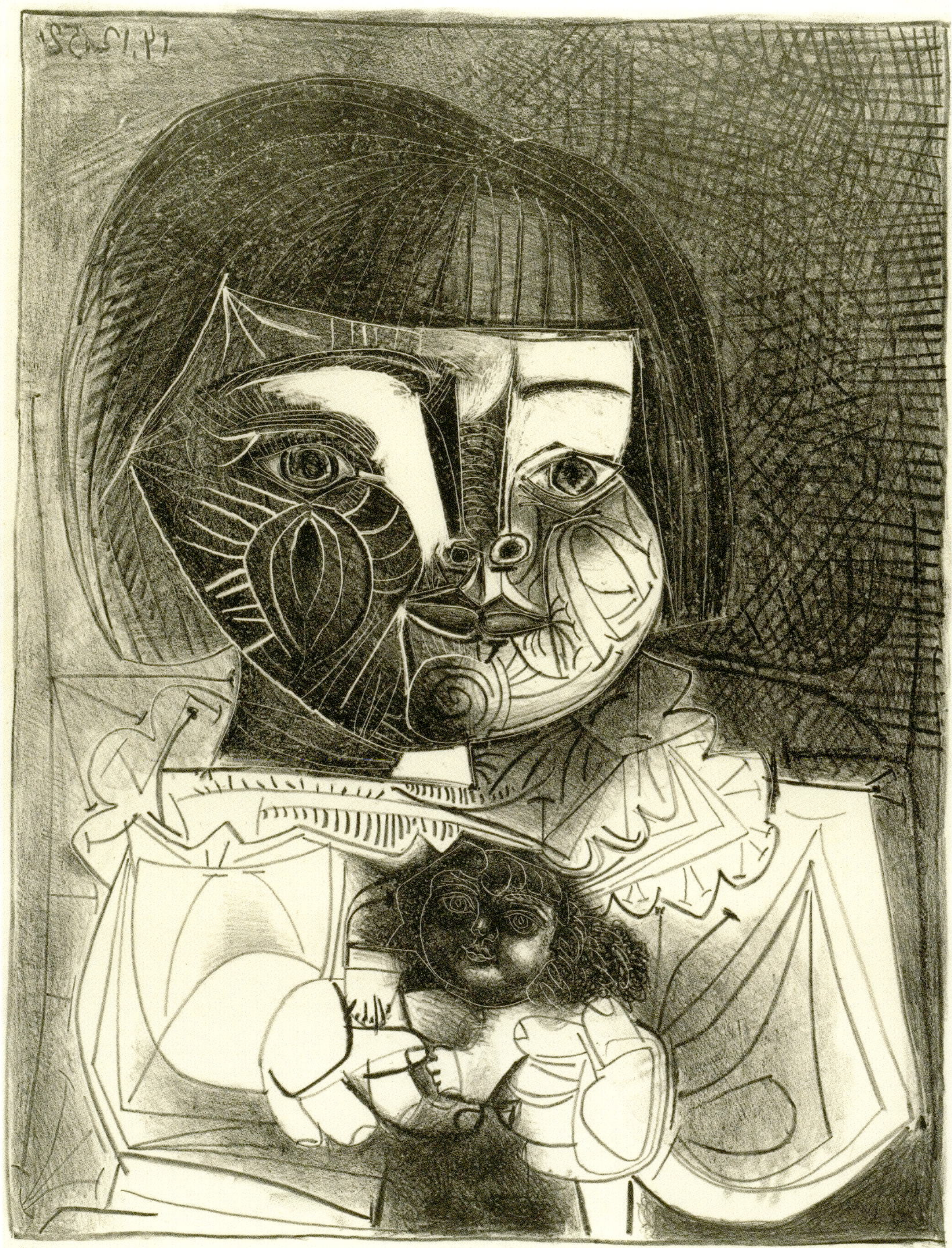

25.
The Italian Woman (after the painting
by Victor Orsel)
1953 (printed 1955)
Lithograph printed from zinc plate
on paper
Image: 17 ½ × 15 in. (44 ½ × 37 cm);
sheet: 25 ⅛ × 19 ½ in. (63.8 × 49.5 cm)
John Szoke Gallery, New York

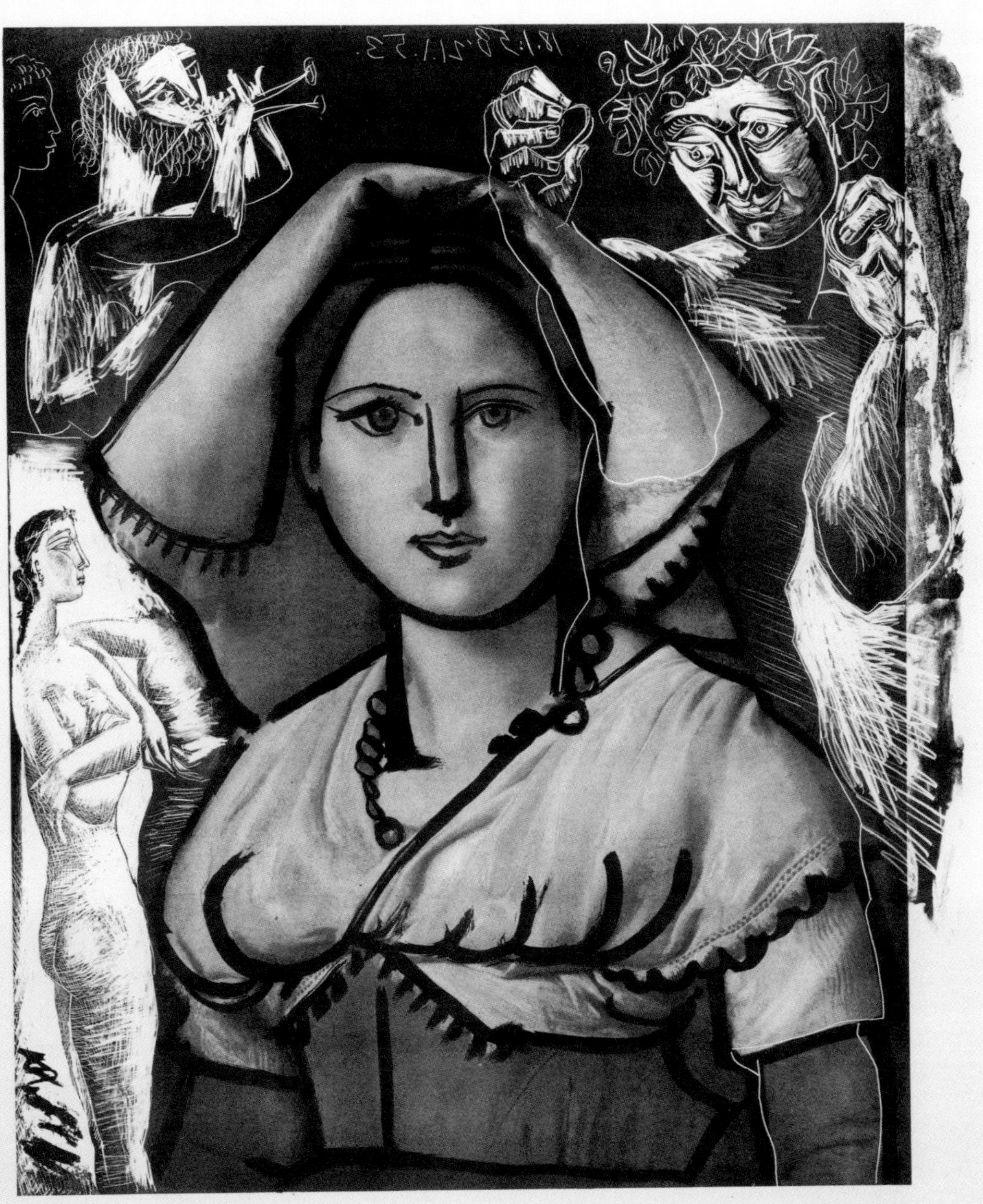

26.
The Egyptian Woman
1953
Sugar-lift aquatint on paper
Image: 32 ⅝ × 18 ⅝ in. (82.9 × 47.3 cm);
sheet: 36 × 25 in. (91.4 × 63.5 cm)
John Szoke Gallery, New York

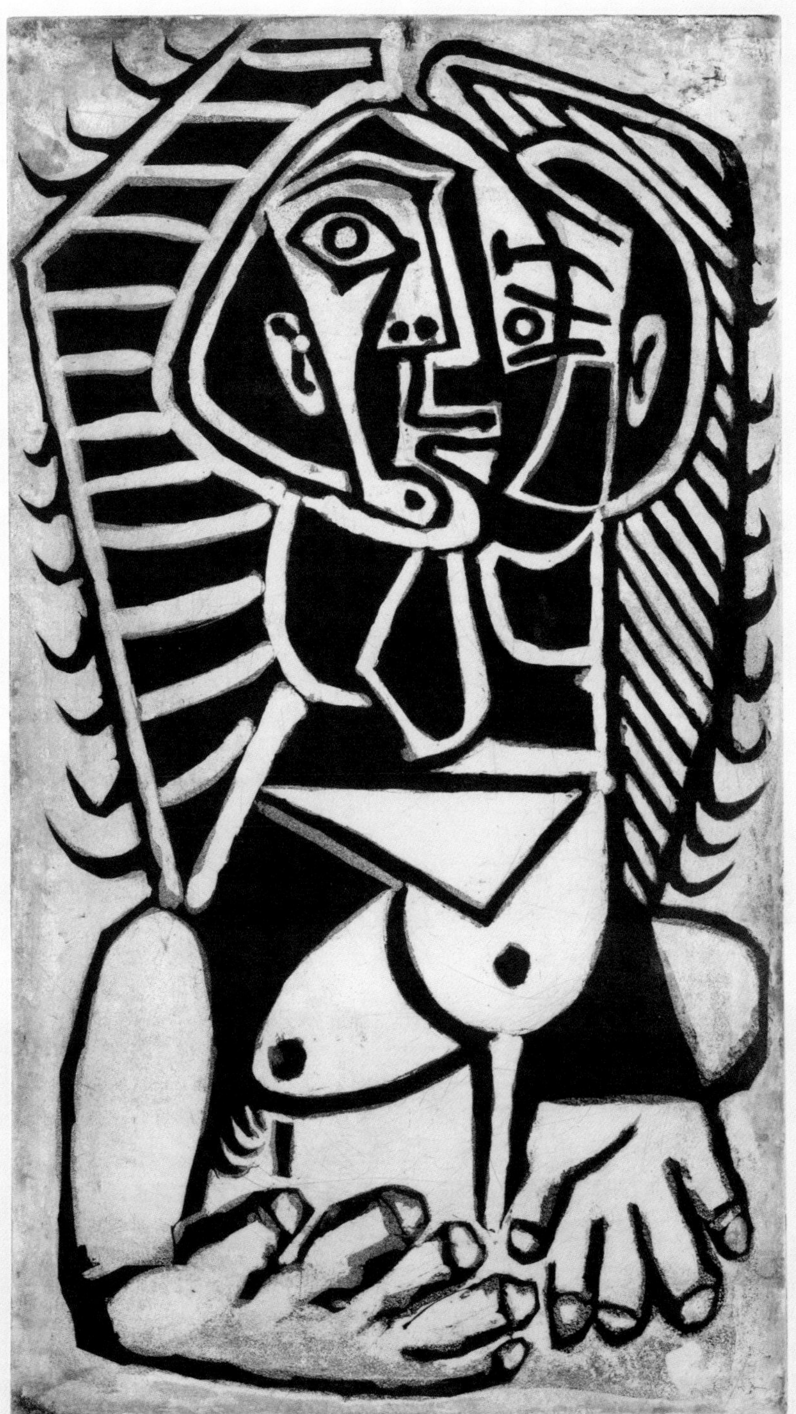

27.
Jacqueline Knitting
1954
Oil on canvas
28 ¾ × 21 ⅝ in. (73 × 54.9 cm)
Private Collection

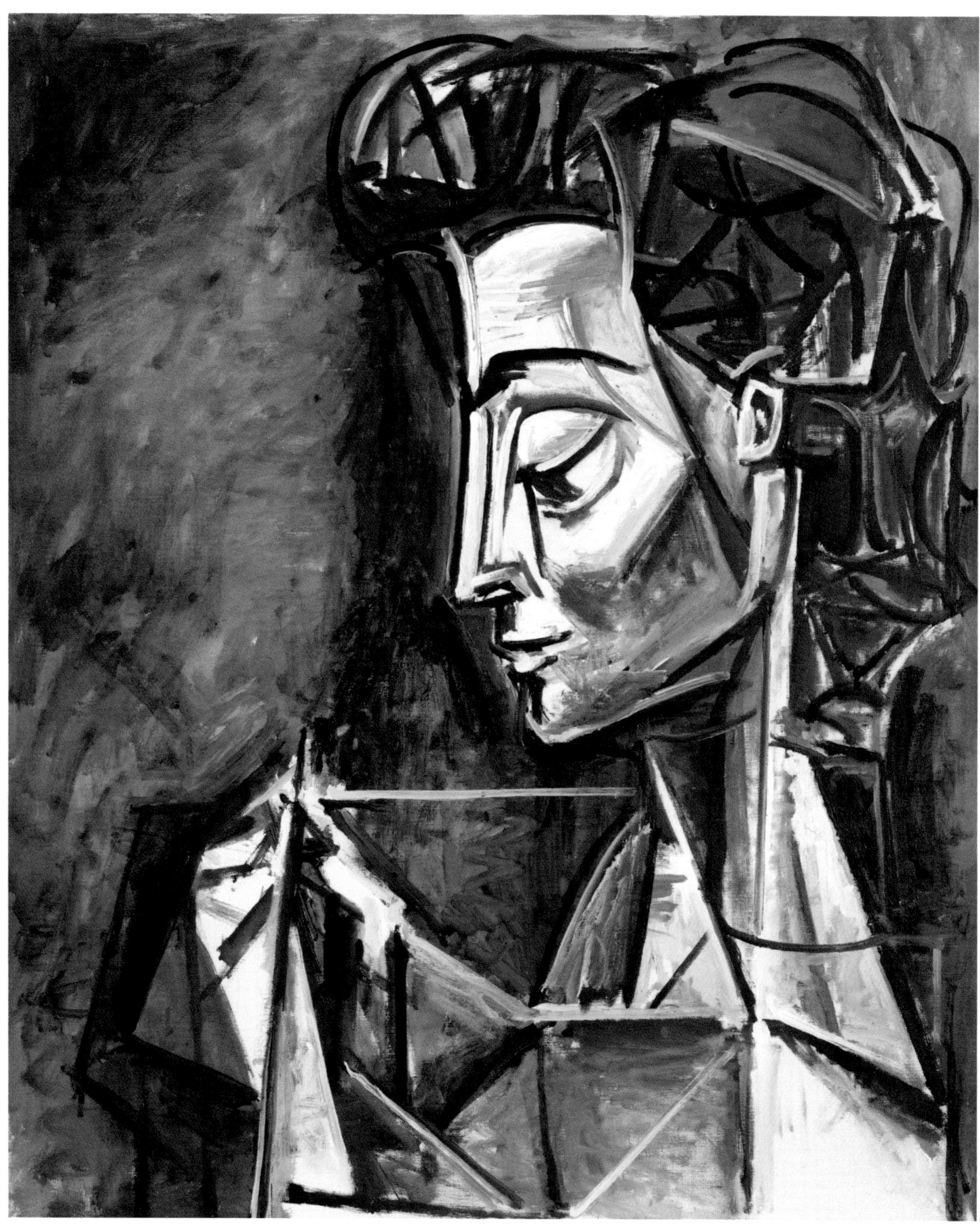

28.
*Portrait of a Young Girl, after Cranach
the Younger, II*
1958
Color linoleum cut on paper
Block: 25 ½ × 21 in. (64.8 × 53.3 cm);
sheet: 30 ½ × 22 ½ in. (77.5 × 57.2 cm)
The Metropolitan Museum of Art,
New York

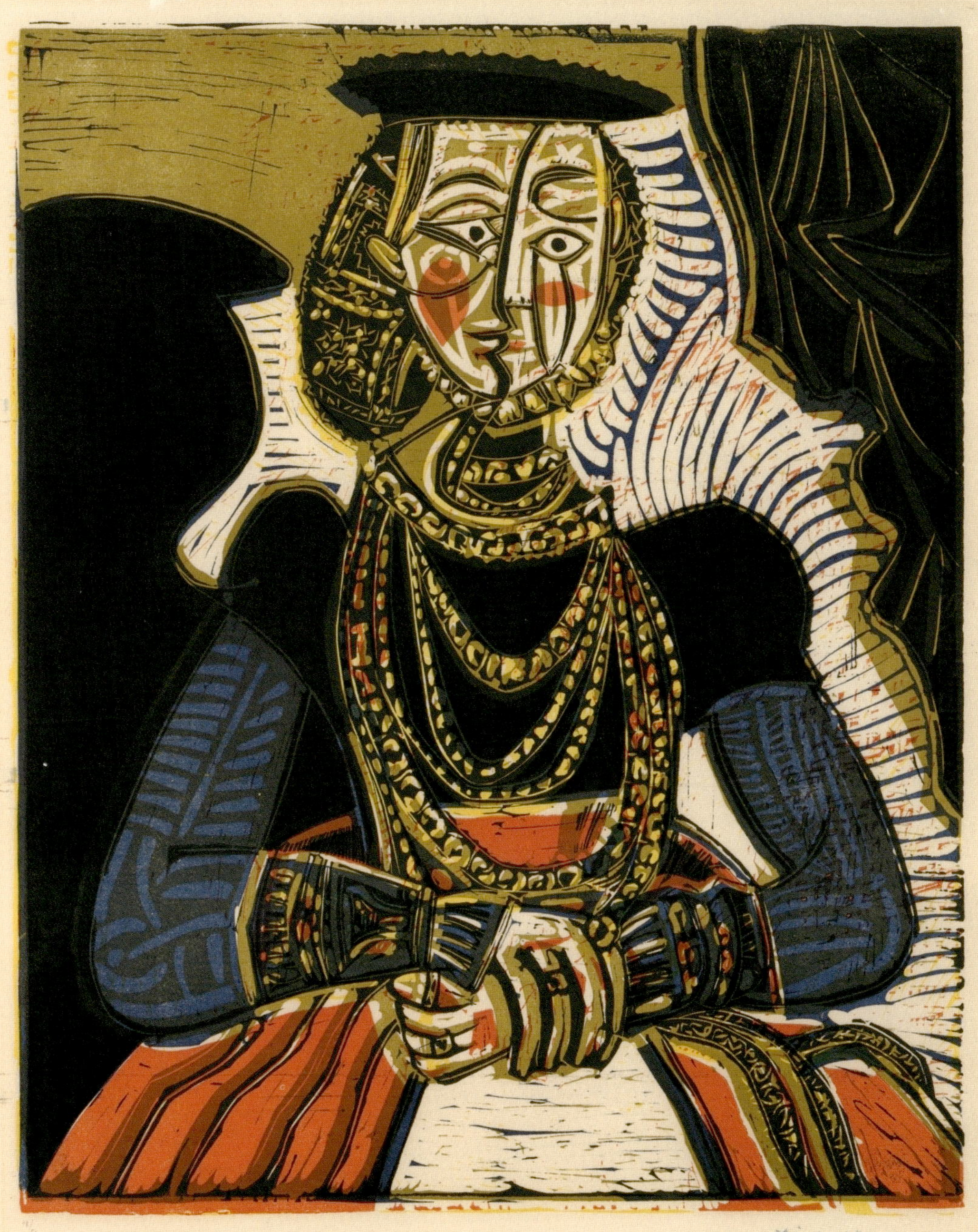

29.
Woman with a Flowered Blouse
1958
Lithograph printed from zinc plate
on paper
Sheet: 25 ⅞ × 19 ¾ in. (65.7 × 50.2 cm)
Private Collection

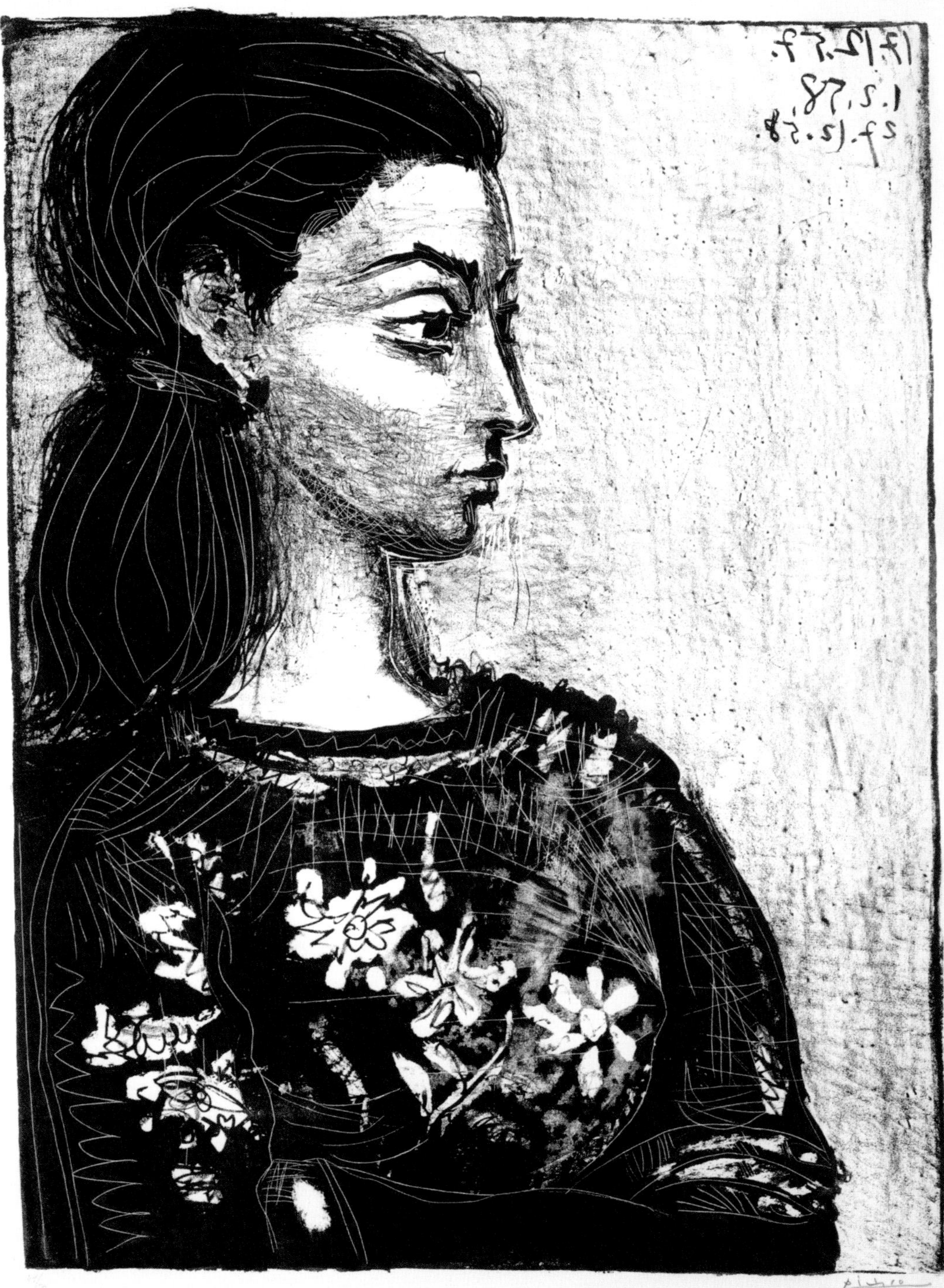

30.
Still Life with Glass Under the Lamp
1962
Color linoleum cut on paper
Block: 20⅞ × 25³⁄₁₆ in. (53 × 64 cm);
sheet: 24½ × 29⅝ in. (62.2 × 75.2 cm)
The Metropolitan Museum of Art,
New York

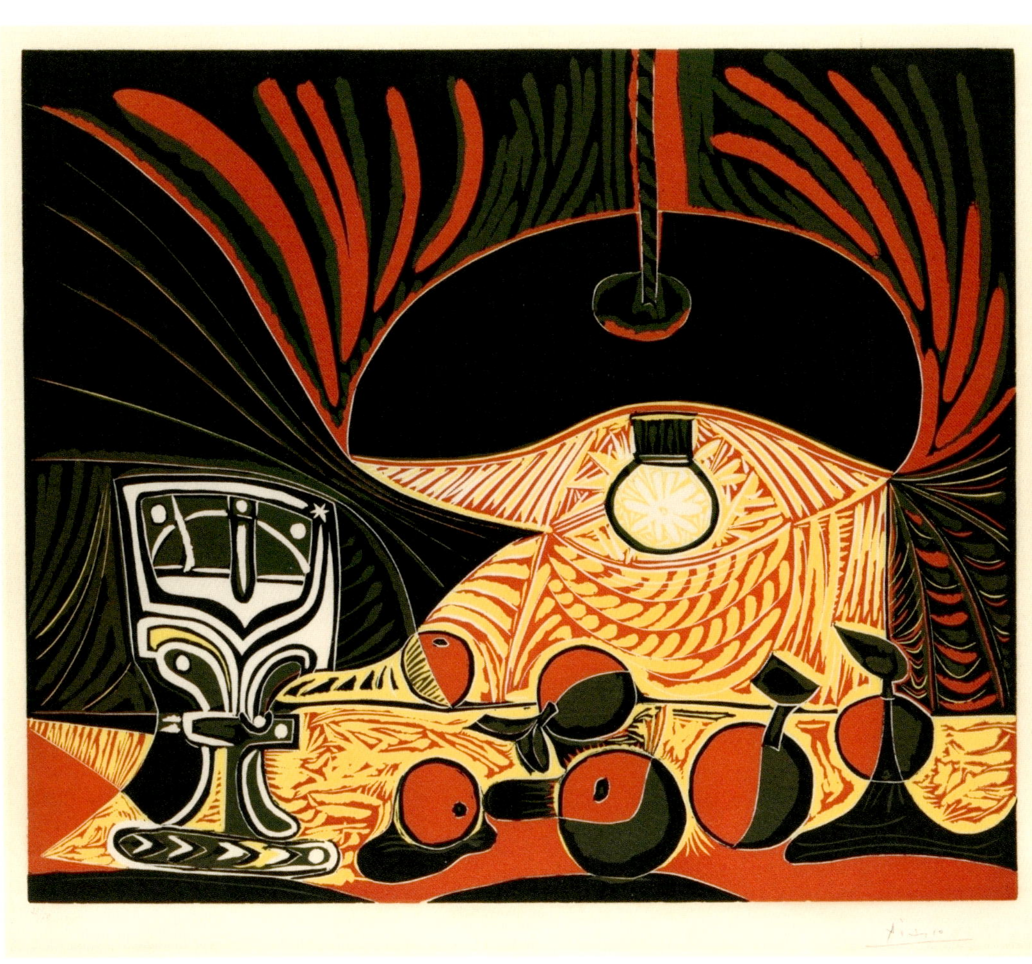

31.
Still Life with Hanging Lamp
1962
Color linoleum cut on paper
Block: 25 ³⁄₁₆ × 20 ¹³⁄₁₆ in. (64 ×
52.9 cm); sheet: 29 ⁵⁄₈ × 24 ½ in.
(75.2 × 62.2 cm)
The Metropolitan Museum of Art,
New York

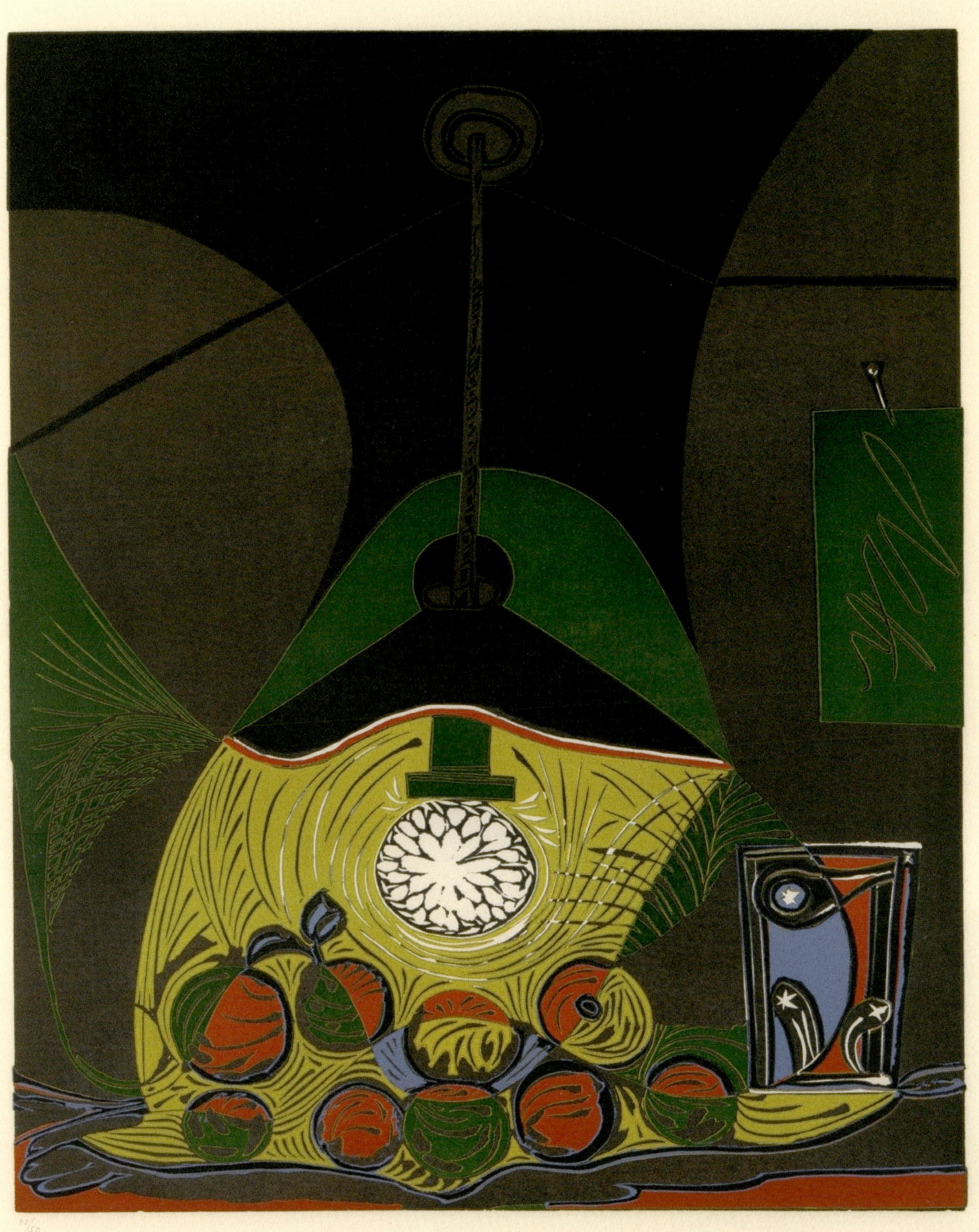

32.
Luncheon on the Grass, after Manet
1968
Color linoleum cut on paper
Image: 20 7/8 × 25 1/8 in. (53 × 64 cm)
Collection of Catherine Woodard
and Nelson Blitz, Jr.

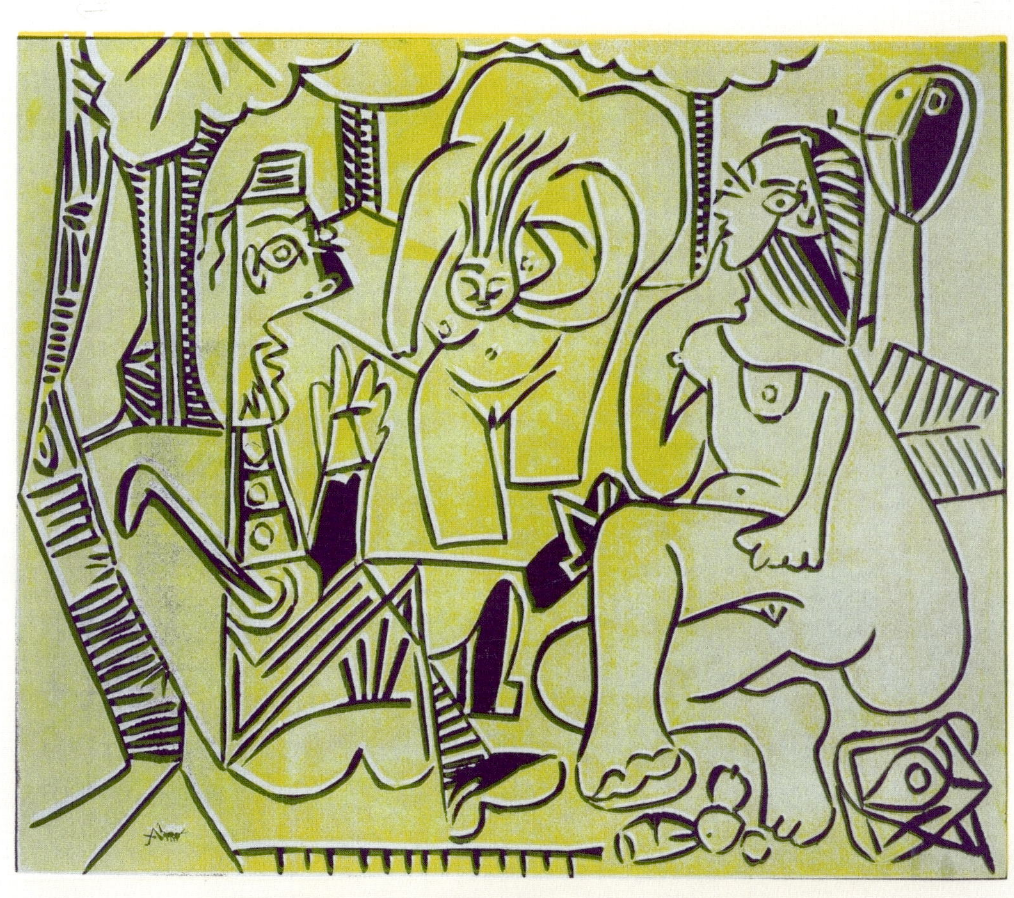

Essai d'un blanc
Le Déjeuner sur l'herbe

33.
Luncheon on the Grass, after Manet
1968
Color linoleum cut on paper
Image: 20 7/8 × 25 1/8 in. (53 × 64 cm)
Collection of Catherine Woodard
and Nelson Blitz, Jr.

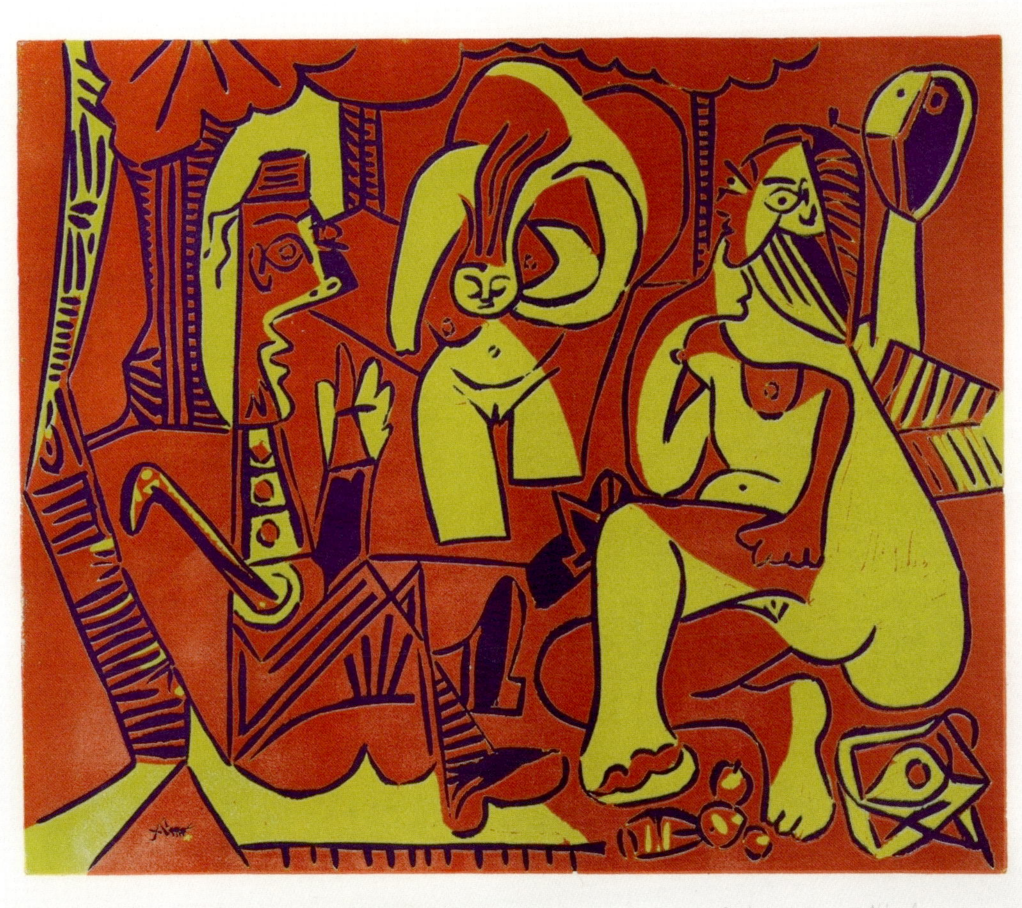
2.62 Ronge épreuve
Le Déjeuner sur l'herbe

34.
Luncheon on the Grass, after Manet
1968
Color linoleum cut on paper
Image: 20 ⅞ × 25 ⅛ in. (53 × 64 cm)
Collection of Catherine Woodard
and Nelson Blitz, Jr.

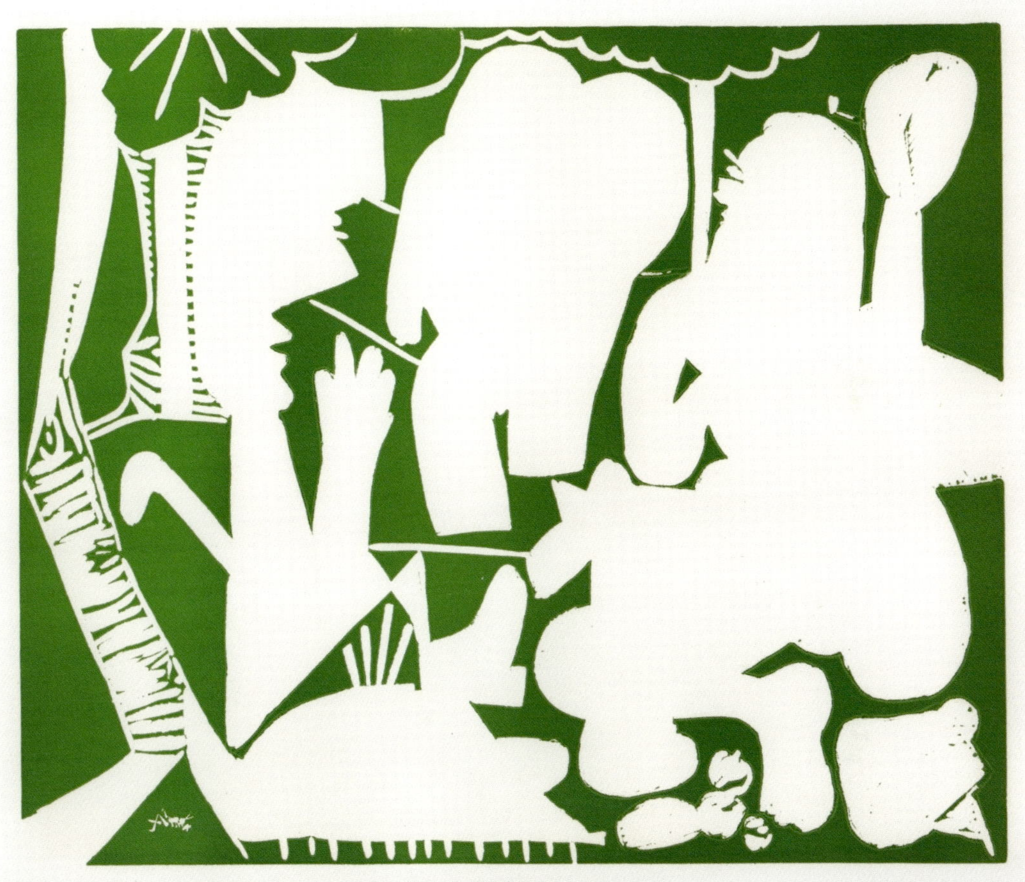

Linogravure de Picasso. 366. Le Déjeuner sur l'herbe 1962 - tirage du ...

35.
Luncheon on the Grass, after Manet
1968
Color linoleum cut on tracing paper
Image: 20⅞ × 25⅛ in. (53 × 64 cm)
Collection of Catherine Woodard
and Nelson Blitz, Jr.

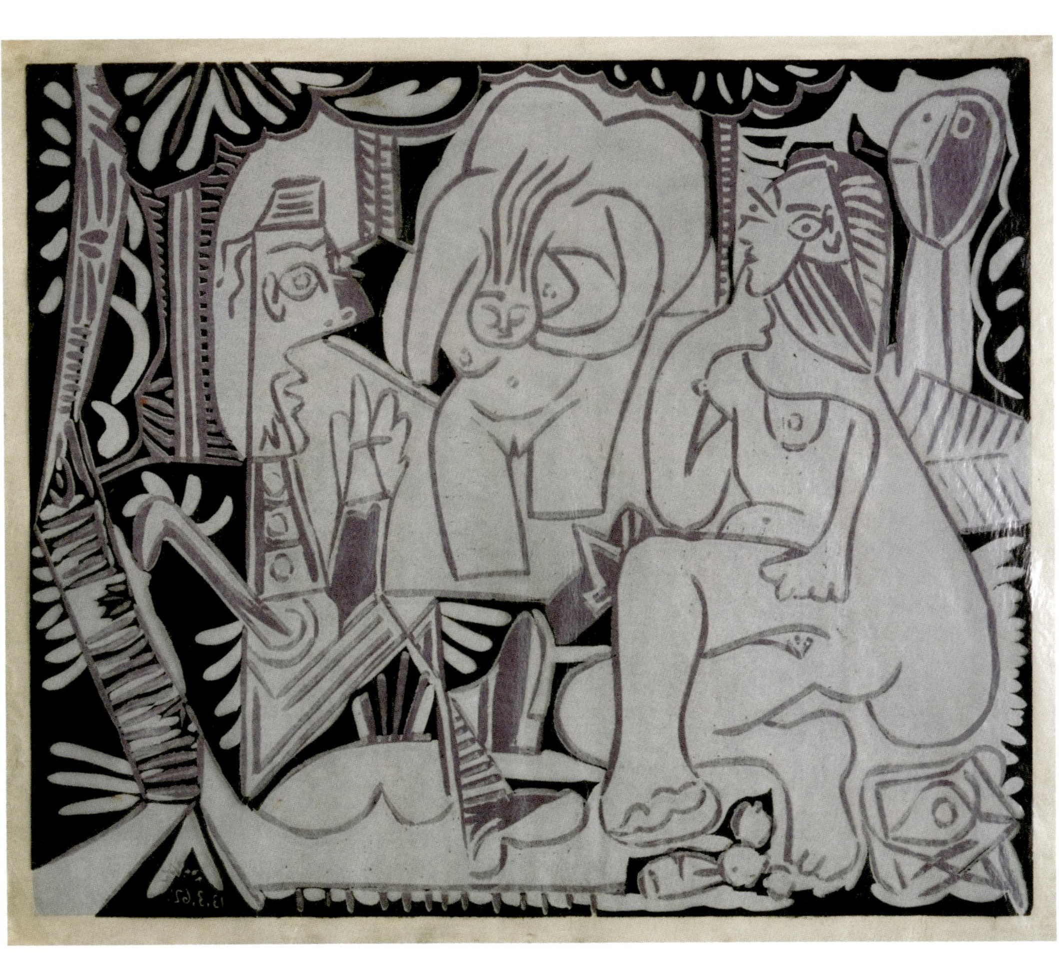

36.
Luncheon on the Grass, after Manet
1968
Color linoleum cut on paper
Image: 20 ⅞ × 25 ⅛ in. (53 × 64 cm)
Collection of Catherine Woodard
and Nelson Blitz, Jr.

Luncheon on the Grass, after Manet
1968
Color linoleum cut on paper
Image: 20 ⅞ × 25 ⅛ in. (53 × 64 cm)
Collection of Catherine Woodard
and Nelson Blitz, Jr.

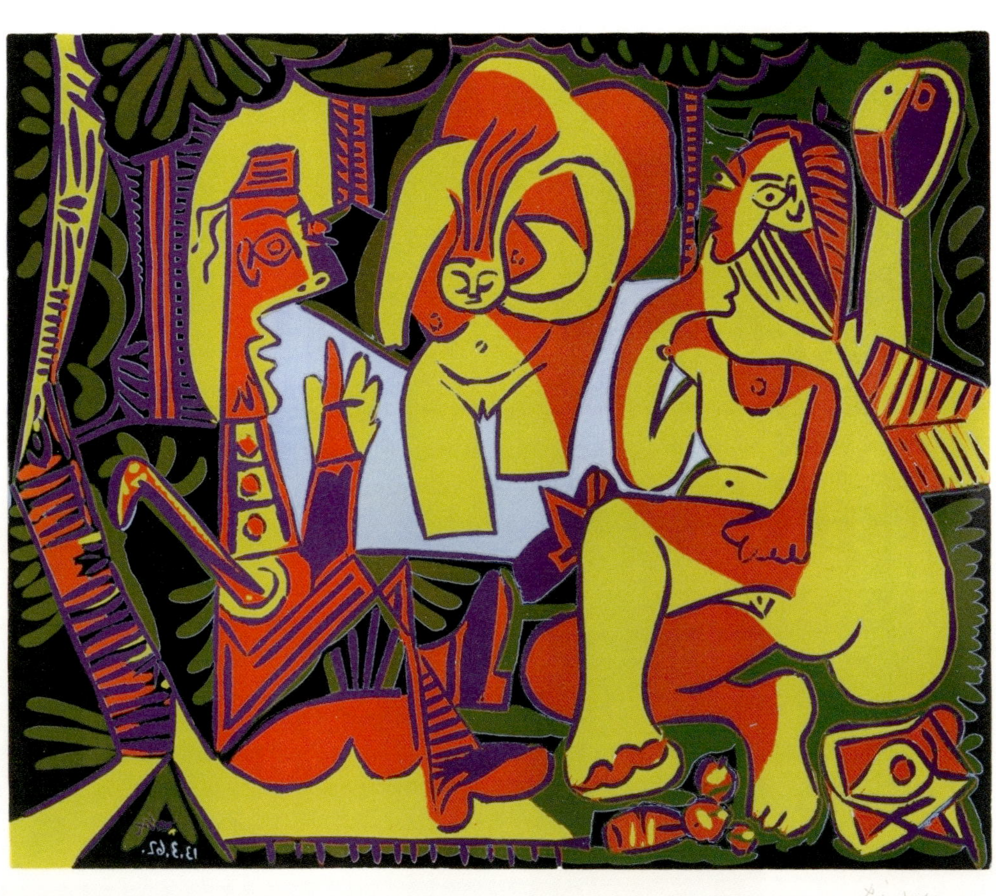

37.
Picasso, His Art and His Public,
from *Suite 347*
1968 (printed 1969)
Etching on paper
Image: 15 ½ × 22 ¼ in. (39.4 ×
56.5 cm); sheet: 22 ½ × 28 in. (57.2 ×
71.1 cm)
John Szoke Gallery, New York

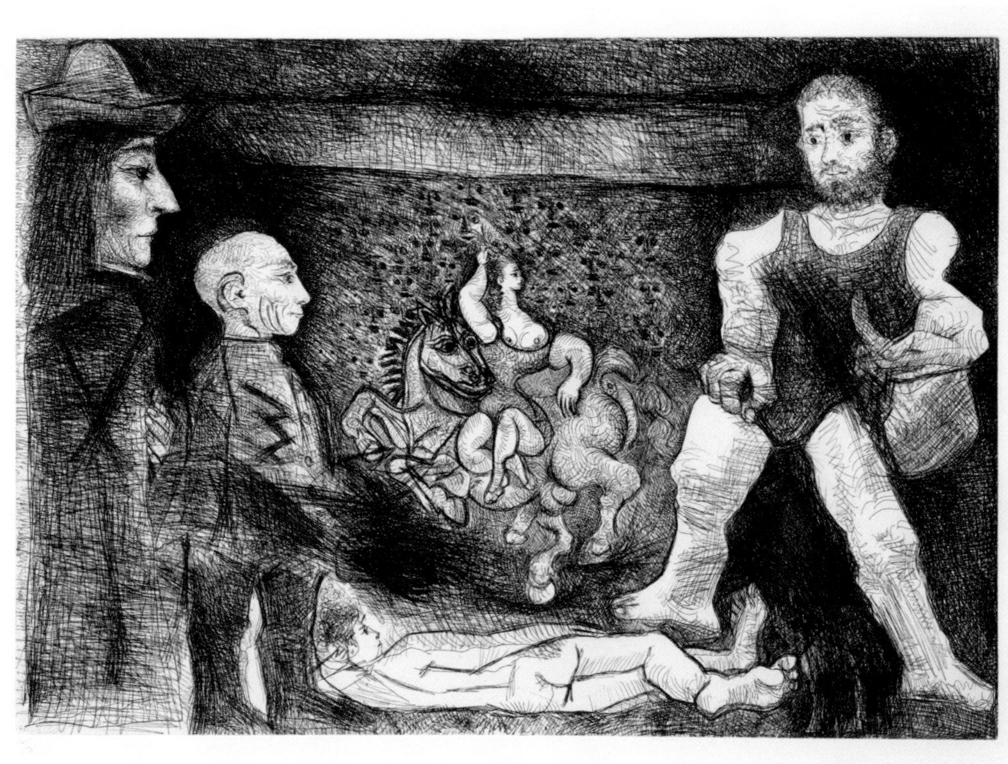

38.
Ecce Homo, after Rembrandt,
from *156 Engravings*
1970 (printed 1975–77)
Etching, aquatint, scraper, and
drypoint on paper
Image: 19 ½ × 16 ¼ in. (49.5 ×
41.3 cm); sheet: 26 7/8 × 22 in.
(68.3 × 55.9 cm)
John Szoke Gallery, New York

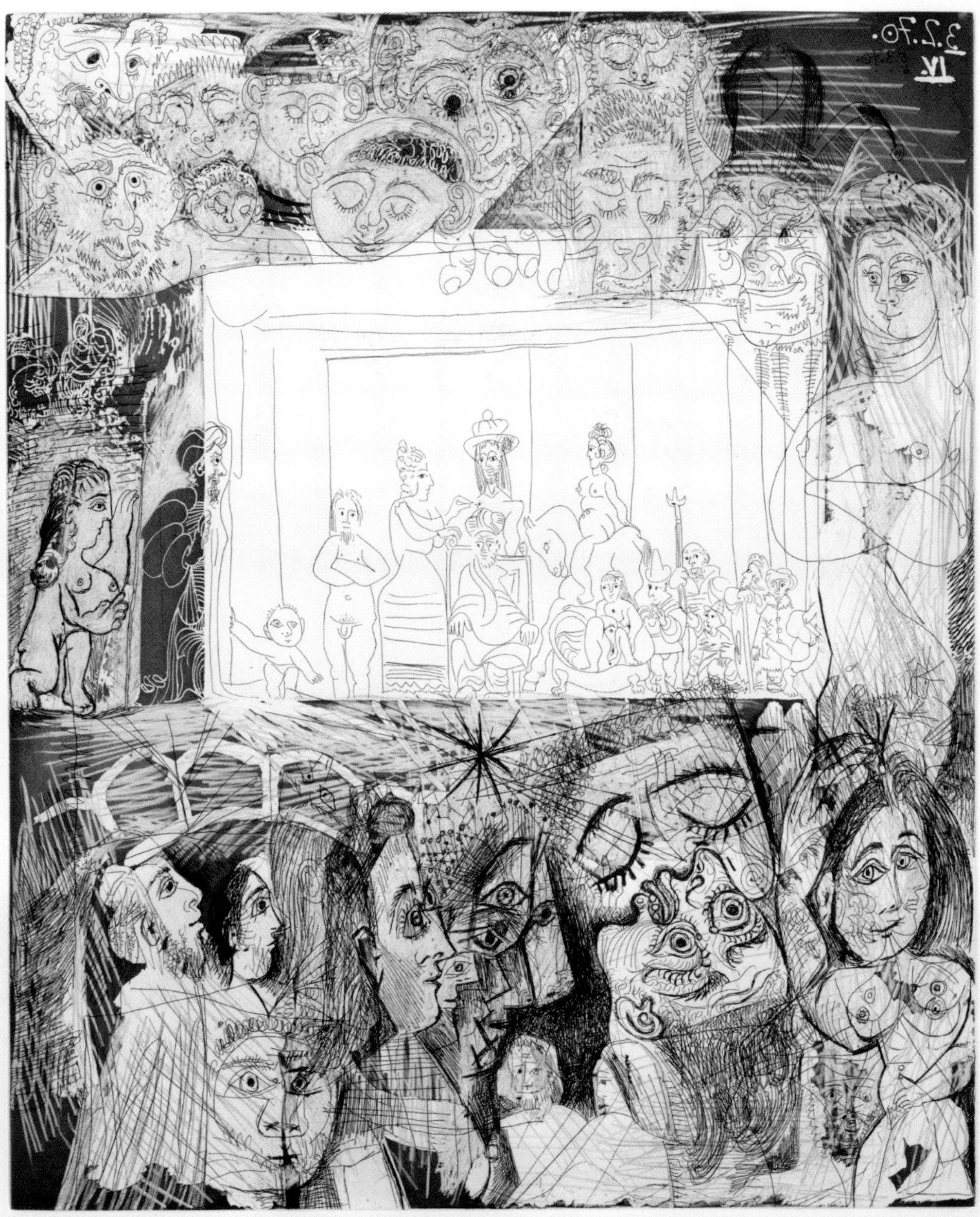

1.
Self-Portrait
Late 1901
Oil on canvas
31 ⅞ × 23 ⅝ in. (81 × 60 cm)
Zervos, volume 1, no. 91
Musée national Picasso-Paris
Pablo Picasso acceptance in lieu, 1979
MP4

2.
The Frugal Repast
1904
Etching on paper
Plate: 18 ⅛ × 14 ⅞ in. (46.1 × 37.8 cm);
sheet: 20 ¹⁵⁄₁₆ × 17 ⁷⁄₁₆ in. (53.2 ×
44.3 cm)
Inscribed in graphite, l.l., below plate:
no. 4; in graphite, l.r., below plate:
Picasso
Printed by Delâtre
Baer 2 I/II
Clark Art Institute, Williamstown,
Massachusetts
Acquired by the Clark, 1962
1962.89

3.
Salomé, from *The Suite of the
Saltimbanques*
1905
Drypoint on paper
Image: 15 ⅞ × 13 ¾ in. (40.3 ×
34.9 cm); sheet: 25 ⅜ × 19 ⅜ in. (64.5 ×
49.2 cm)
Inscribed u.r., within plate:
Picasso/1905; in graphite, l.r., below
plate: *Picasso/1905*
Printed by Delâtre
Baer 17 I/III.a
John Szoke Gallery, New York

4.
*Bust of a Young Woman (Fernande
Olivier)*
1906 (printed 1933)
Woodcut on paper
Image and sheet: 19 ¼ × 14 in. (48.9 ×
35.6 cm)
Inscribed in graphite, l.r., within plate:
3/15 Picasso; in graphite, u.l., within
plate: *8 janvier XXXIII*
Printed by the artist
Baer 212 only state
Collection of Catherine Woodard and
Nelson Blitz, Jr.

5.
Still Life with Bottle of Marc
1912
Drypoint on paper
Plate: 19 ⅝ × 12 in. (49.8 × 30.5 cm);
sheet: 28 ⅜ × 21 ⅝ in. (72.1 × 54.9 cm)
Inscribed in graphite, u.l., above plate:
40.000, 7258; in graphite, u.r., above
plate: *13249*; in graphite, l.r., below
plate: *Maeght 9840*
Printed by Delâtre
Baer 33 I/I.b
Philadelphia Museum of Art
125th Anniversary Acquisition, Gift of
the Judith Rothschild Foundation, 2007
2007-46-16

6.
Portrait of Olga in a Fur Collar
1923 (printed 1955)
Drypoint on paper
Plate: 19 ½ × 19 ⅜ in. (49.5 × 49.2 cm)
Printed by Fort
Baer 109 only state
Collection of Catherine Woodard and
Nelson Blitz, Jr.

7.
Visage (Face of Marie-Thérèse)
1928
Lithograph on chine collé, laid down on
paper
Image: 8 × 5 ⅝ in. (20.3 × 14.3 cm);
sheet: 10 ¼ × 8 ⅜ in. (26 × 21.3 cm)
Printed by Marchizer
Inscribed in graphite, l.r., below plate:
Picasso; in graphite, l.l., below plate:
8/25
Mourlot 23 only state
John Szoke Gallery, New York

8.
Two Clothed Models, from *The Vollard
Suite*
1933 (printed 1939)
Etching on paper
Plate: 10 ½ × 7 ⁹⁄₁₆ in. (26.7 × 19.2 cm);
sheet: 17 ½ × 13 ¼ in. (44.4 × 33.7 cm)
Printed by Lacourière
Inscribed in graphite, l.r., below plate:
Picasso; l.r., within plate: *PARIS 21 mars
XXXIII*
Baer 302 II/II.c
Clark Art Institute, Williamstown,
Massachusetts
Gift of William and Ann Roberts with
George and Laura Estes, 1998
1998.34

9.
Large Bullfight, with Female Bullfighter
1934 (printed 1939)
Etching on paper
Plate: 19 7/16 × 27 1/16 in. (49.4 ×
68.7 cm); sheet: 22 3/16 × 30 1/4 in.
(56.3 × 76.8 cm)
Inscribed in graphite, l.l., below plate:
1e etat; l.r., within plate: *Boisegeloup
8 septembre XXXIV*; in graphite, l.r.,
below plate: *Picasso*
Printed by Lacourière
Baer 433 only state
Museum of Modern Art, New York
Acquired through the Lillie P. Bliss
Bequest
244.1947

10.
Blind Minotaur Led by a Young Girl
1934
Aquatint, engraving, and drypoint on
paper
Plate: 9 11/16 × 13 11/16 in. (24.6 ×
34.8 cm); sheet: 13 1/8 × 17 1/2 in. (33.4 ×
44.5 cm)
Inscribed in graphite, l.r., below plate:
Picasso
Printed by Lacourière
Baer 437 IV/IV.b
Museum of Fine Arts, Boston
Frederic Brown Fund
56.151

11.
Minotauromachia
1935 (printed 1936)
Etching and engraving on paper
Plate: 19 1/2 × 27 1/4 in. (49.5 × 69.2 cm);
sheet: 22 1/4 × 30 in. (56.5 × 76.2 cm)
Inscribed in ink, l.l., below plate: *2/50*;
in pencil, l.r., below plate: *Picasso*
Printed by Lacourière
Baer 573 VII/VII.c.3
Private Collection

12.
*Faun Unveiling a Sleeping Girl (Jupiter
and Antiope, after Rembrandt)*, from
The Vollard Suite
1936 (printed 1939)
Aquatint and sugar-lift aquatint,
engraving, and scraper on paper
Image: 12 1/2 × 16 1/4 in. (31.8 ×
41.3 cm); sheet: 15 1/4 × 19 1/2 in. (38.7 ×
49.5 cm)
Inscribed in graphite, l.l., below plate:
.387; inscribed in pencil, l.r., below
plate: *Picasso*; inscribed l.r., in plate:
Paris, 12 juin VI
Printed by Lacourière
Baer 609 VI/VI.B.c
Collection of Catherine Woodard and
Nelson Blitz, Jr.

13.
Portrait of Dora Maar
1937
Oil on canvas
36 1/4 × 25 5/8 in. (92 × 65 cm)
Zervos, volume 8, no. 331
Musée national Picasso-Paris
Pablo Picasso acceptance in lieu, 1979
MP158

14.
The Weeping Woman, I
1937
Drypoint, aquatint, etching, and scraper
on paper
Plate: 27 1/8 × 19 1/2 in. (68.9 × 49.5 cm);
sheet: 30 5/16 × 22 5/16 in. (77 × 56.7 cm)
Inscribed in graphite, l.l., below plate:
12/15; in graphite, l.r., below plate:
Picasso
Printed by Lacourière
Baer 623 III/VII.b
Museum of Modern Art, New York
Acquired through the generosity of the
Katsko Suzuki Memorial Fund, the Riva
Castleman Endowment Fund, David
Rockefeller, The Philip and Lynn Straus
Foundation Fund, and Agnes Gund and
Daniel Shapiro; Linda and Bill Goldstein,
Mr. and Mrs. Herbert D. Schimmel, the
Edward John Noble Foundation, and
the Associates of the Department of
Prints and Illustrated Books; The Cowles
Charitable Trust, Nelson Blitz, Jr. with
Catherine Woodard and Perri and
Allison Blitz, Mary Ellen Meehan, and
Anna Marie and Robert F. Shapiro; and
Ruth and Louis Aledort, Carol and Bert
Freidus, David S. Orentreich, M.D., and
Susan and Peter Ralston
445.1999

15.
The Weeping Woman, I
1937
Drypoint, aquatint, etching, and scraper
on paper
Image: 27 1/8 × 19 3/8 in. (68.9 ×
49.2 cm); sheet: 30 1/2 × 25 5/8 in. (77.5 ×
65.1 cm)
Inscribed in graphite, l.l., below plate:
8/15; inscribed in graphite, l.r., below
plate: *Picasso*
Printed by Lacourière
Baer 623 VII/VII.A.b
Private Collection

16.
The Weeping Woman, III
1937
Drypoint, aquatint, and foul-biting on
paper
Plate: 13 5/8 × 9 5/8 in. (34.6 × 24.6 cm)
Inscribed u.r., within the plate: *4 juillet
37 (I)*
Printed by Frélaut
Baer 625 A
Collection of Catherine Woodard and
Nelson Blitz, Jr.

17.
The Weeping Woman, IV
1937
Drypoint on paper
Plate: 13 5/8 × 9 7/8 in. (34.7 × 25 cm)
Inscribed u.r., within the plate: *4 juillet
37 (II)*
Printed by Frélaut
Baer 626 A
Collection of Catherine Woodard and
Nelson Blitz, Jr.

18.
Woman with Tambourine
1939 (printed 1943)
Etching, aquatint, and scraper on paper
Image: 26 1/8 × 20 1/8 in. (66.4 ×
51.1 cm); sheet: 31 × 22 3/8 in. (78.7 ×
56.8 cm)
Inscribed in graphite, l.l., below plate:
8/30 Picasso
Printed by Lacourière
Baer 646 V/V.B.a
Private Collection

19.
David and Bathsheba
1947
Lithograph printed from zinc plate on
paper
Image: 25 ³⁄₁₆ × 19 ⁵⁄₁₆ in. (64 × 49 cm);
sheet: 25 ⅞ × 19 ⁹⁄₁₆ in. (65.8 × 49.7 cm)
Inscribed in graphite, l.l., within plate:
49/50; in pencil, l.r., within plate:
Picasso
Printed by Mourlot
Mourlot 109 1ˢᵗ state
Museum of Fine Arts, Boston
Fund in memory of Horatio Greenough
Curtis
56.1192

20.
David and Bathsheba
1949
Lithograph on paper
Image: 25 ¹¹⁄₁₆ × 19 ¹⁄₁₆ in. (65.3 ×
48.4 cm); sheet: 29 ¹⁵⁄₁₆ × 22 in. (76 ×
55.9 cm)
Inscribed in graphite, l.l., below plate:
32/50; in blue, yellow, red, and pink
pencil, l.r., below plate: *Picasso*
Printed by Mourlot
Mourlot 109 bis
Museum of Fine Arts, Boston
Lee M. Friedman Fund
63.1366

21.
The Dove
1949
Lithograph printed from zinc plate
on paper
Composition: 21 ½ × 27 ⁷⁄₁₆ in. (54.4 ×
70 cm); sheet: 22 × 30 in. (55.9 ×
76.2 cm)
Inscribed in graphite, l.l., outside plate:
24/50; in graphite, l.r., outside plate:
Picasso
Printed by Mourlot
Mourlot 141 only state
Philadelphia Museum of Art
Gift of the Philadelphia Water Color
Club, 1950
1950.7.1

22.
Venus and Cupid, after Cranach
1949 and 1951
Aquatint, scraper, burin and drypoint on
paper
Image: 31 ⅜ × 16 ⅞ in. (79.7 ×
42.9 cm); sheet: 35 ½ × 25 in. (90.2 ×
63.5 cm)
Printed by Frélaut
Baer 876 VI/VI.A.a
John Szoke Gallery, New York

23.
Woman at the Window
1952
Sugar-lift aquatint on paper
Plate: 32 ⅞ × 18 ⅝ in. (83.5 × 47.3 cm)
Printed by Lacourière
Baer 891 II/II.A
Collection of Catherine Woodard and
Nelson Blitz, Jr.

24.
*Paloma and Her Doll on Black
Background*
1952
Lithograph printed from zinc plate on
paper
Composition: 27 ¹¹⁄₁₆ × 21 ¾ in. (70.4 ×
55.3 cm); sheet: 29 ½ × 22 ³⁄₁₆ in. (75 ×
56.3 cm)
Printed by Mourlot
Inscribed in graphite, l.l., outside plate:
30/50; in red pencil, l.r., outside plate:
Picasso; u.r., within plate: *14.12.52*
Mourlot 229 only state
Museum of Modern Art, New York
Curt Valentin Bequest
366.1955

25.
*The Italian Woman (after the painting
by Victor Orsel)*
1953 (printed 1955)
Lithograph printed from zinc plate on
paper
Image: 17 ½ × 15 in. (44 ½ × 37 cm);
sheet: 25 ⅛ × 19 ½ in. (63.8 × 49.5 cm)
Inscribed in graphite, l.l., below plate:
13/50; in pencil, l.r., below plate:
Picasso
Printed by Mourlot
Mourlot 238 2ⁿᵈ state
John Szoke Gallery, New York

26.
The Egyptian Woman
1953
Sugar-lift aquatint on paper
Image: 32 ⅝ × 18 ⅝ in. (82.9 ×
47.3 cm); sheet: 36 × 25 in. (91.4 ×
63.5 cm)
Inscribed in graphite, l.l., below plate:
30/50; in ink, l.r., below plate: *Picasso*
Printed by Lacourière
Baer 906 II/II.B.b.1
John Szoke Gallery, New York

27.
Jacqueline Knitting
1954
Oil on canvas
28 ¾ × 21 ⅝ in. (73 × 54.9 cm)
Private Collection

28.
*Portrait of a Young Girl, after Cranach
the Younger, II*
1958
Color linoleum cut on paper
Block: 25 ½ × 21 in. (64.8 × 53.3 cm);
sheet: 30 ½ × 22 ½ in. (77.5 × 57.2 cm)
Inscribed in graphite, l.l., below plate:
18/50; in blue pencil, l.r., below plate:
Picasso
Printed by Hidalgo Arnéra
Baer 1053 i/i.C.a
The Metropolitan Museum of Art,
New York
The Mr. and Mrs. Charles Kramer
Collection, Gift of Mr. and Mrs. Charles
Kramer, 1985
1985.1079.1

29.
Woman with a Flowered Blouse
1957–58
Lithograph printed from zinc plate
on paper
Sheet: 25 ⅞ × 19 ¾ in. (65.7 × 50.2 cm)
Inscribed u.r., in stone:
17.12.57/1.2.58/27.12.58; in graphite,
l.r., below stone: *Picasso*
Printed by Mourlot
Mourlot 307 3ʳᵈ state
Private Collection

30.
Still Life with Glass Under the Lamp
1962
Color linoleum cut on paper
Block: 20 ⅞ × 25 ³⁄₁₆ in. (53 × 64 cm);
sheet: 24 ½ × 29 ⅝ in. (62.2 × 75.2 cm)
Inscribed in graphite, l.l., below image:
33/50; in graphite, l.r., below image:
Picasso
Printed by Hidalgo Arnéra
Baer 1312 V/V.B.a
The Metropolitan Museum of Art, New
York
The Mr. and Mrs. Charles Kramer
Collection, Gift of Mr. and Mrs. Charles
Kramer, 1979
1979.620.90

31.
Still Life with Hanging Lamp
1962
Color linoleum cut on paper
Block: 25 ³⁄₁₆ × 20 ¹³⁄₁₆ in. (64 × 52.9 cm);
sheet: 29 ⅝ × 24 ½ in. (75.2 × 62.2 cm)
Inscribed in graphite, l.l., below image:
43/50; in graphite, l.r., below image:
Picasso
Printed by Hidalgo Arnéra
Baer 1313 I/I.B.g.2.a
The Metropolitan Museum of Art,
New York
The Mr. and Mrs. Charles Kramer
Collection, Gift of Mr. and Mrs. Charles
Kramer, 1979
1979.620.91

32.
Luncheon on the Grass, after Manet
1968
Color linoleum cut on paper
Image: 20 ⅞ × 25 ⅛ in. (53 × 64 cm)
Inscribed in graphite, by printer, l.r.:
1962/Essai d'un blanc; in graphite, l.r.:
Le Déjeuner sur l'herbe
Printed by Hidalgo Arnéra
Baer 1287 I/V
Collection of Catherine Woodard and
Nelson Blitz, Jr.

33.
Luncheon on the Grass, after Manet
1968
Color linoleum cut on paper
Image: 20 ⅞ × 25 ⅛ in. (53 × 64 cm)
Inscribed in graphite, by printer, l.l.:
2.62 Rouge épreuve; in graphite, l.r.:
Le Déjeuner sur l'herbe
Printed by Hidalgo Arnéra
Baer 1287 II/V
Collection of Catherine Woodard and
Nelson Blitz, Jr.

34.
Luncheon on the Grass, after Manet
1968
Color linoleum cut on paper
Image: 20 ⅞ × 25 ⅛ in. (53 × 64 cm)
Inscribed in graphite, by printer, l.l.:
*Linogravure du Picasso .366 Le
Dejeuner sur l'herbe. 1962. Tirage du
vert*
Printed by Hidalgo Arnéra
Baer 1287 III/V
Collection of Catherine Woodard and
Nelson Blitz, Jr.

35.
Luncheon on the Grass, after Manet
1968
Color linoleum cut on tracing paper
Image: 20 ⅞ × 25 ⅛ in. (53 × 64 cm)
Inscribed, l.l., in block: *13.3.62*
Printed by Hidalgo Arnéra
Baer 1287 V/V
Collection of Catherine Woodard and
Nelson Blitz, Jr.

36.
Luncheon on the Grass, after Manet
1968
Color linoleum cut on paper
Image: 20 ⅞ × 25 ⅛ in. (53 × 64 cm)
Inscribed l.l., in block: *13.3.62*; in
graphite, l.r.: *Picasso*
Printed by Hidalgo Arnéra
Baer 1287 V/V.B.b
Collection of Catherine Woodard and
Nelson Blitz, Jr.

37.
Picasso, His Art and His Public,
from *Suite 347*
1968 (printed 1969)
Etching on paper
Image: 15 ½ × 22 ¼ in. (39.4 ×
56.5 cm); sheet: 22 ½ × 28 in. (57.2 ×
71.1 cm)
Inscribed in graphite, l.l., below plate:
37/50; in graphite, l.r., below plate:
Picasso
Printed by Crommelynck
Baer 1496 VII/VII.B.b.1
John Szoke Gallery, New York

38.
Ecce Homo, after Rembrandt, from
156 Engravings
1970 (printed 1975–77)
Etching, aquatint, scraper, and drypoint
on paper
Image: 19 ½ × 16 ¼ in. (49.5 ×
41.3 cm); sheet: 26 ⅞ × 22 in. (68.3 ×
55.9 cm)
Inscribed u.r., within plate: *3.2.70/VI*;
in graphite, l.l., below plate: *29/50*;
stamped, l.r., below plate: *Picasso*
Printed by Crommelynck
Baer 1870 V/V.B.a
John Szoke Gallery, New York

CONTRIBUTORS

Jay A. Clarke is Manton Curator of Prints, Drawings, and Photographs at the Clark Art Institute and a lecturer in the Graduate Program in the History of Art at Williams College. Her publications include *Becoming Edvard Munch: Influence, Anxiety, and Myth* (2009) and essays on the critical reception of Käthe Kollwitz and Max Beckmann, Munch's use of repetition, and Julius Meier-Graefe as an art dealer. She edited and contributed to *Innovation, Tradition and Nostalgia: The Manton Collection of British Art* (2012), *The Impressionist Line from Degas to Toulouse-Lautrec* (2013), and *Machine Age Modernism: Prints from the Daniel Cowin Collection* (2015).

Marilyn McCully is an internationally recognized Picasso expert, based in London. She has organized numerous exhibitions and written widely about Picasso and his background in Spain. Her most recent exhibitions include *Picasso Côte d'Azur* (Monte Carlo: Grimaldi Forum, 2013) and *Picasso in Holland* (Alkmaar City Museum, 2015). Dr. McCully is currently preparing a book on Picasso's correspondence and writings, which will be translated into English.